Karisa Moore draws from the marrow of her personal pain to craft healing for those afflicted by tragedy. *Turn the Page: Devotions to Help the Griever Hope* shares practical wisdom aligned with insights therapists might offer to those who mourn. Moore weaves brief devotions to bandage the hearts of those who cannot endure long passages. She ties her daily messages with small steps toward hope, demonstrating compassion in the white space on every page. Moore's devotional has the potential to bless readers with its caring structure and content. I recommend Karisa Moore's heart-crafted book as a daily dose of comfort to those who've experienced loss.

—Tina Yeager, LMHC
life coach, award-winning author, speaker, and host of
"Flourish-Meant" and "Flourish Today" media shows.

Turn the Page made me reflect and cry, and I can see it taking us on the path to healing.

—Dr. Katherine Hutchinson-Hayes
speaker, podcaster, editor, and author of *Dressing in God's Love Through the Spoken & Written Word*

"You never get over losing a child," has become a hollow cliché that gives no hope to grieving parents. Karisa Moore acknowledges the profound pain of loss, as only one who has experienced the unthinkable can, as she gently leads the reader to walk beside her and experience the peace that only God can bring to the brokenhearted.

— Rhonda Robinson
award-winning author of *FreeFall: Holding onto Faith When the Unthinkable Strikes*

High praise for this 60-day devotional that you will want to read over and over for the next 305 days and beyond. Karisa paints a vivid picture of the waves of emotions experienced during grief. Her words are crafted with care and compassion. It is filled with hope, help, and healing from a biblical perspective based on processing the pain of loss and the joys of life. The book is courageous, comforting, and captivating.

—Dr. Sabrina Black
counselor, professor, international speaker, and author of *Living Right Now* and *Can Two Walk Together*

Wherever you are in your grief journey, turn the page to read Karisa Moore's hope-fueled devotional. Let *Turn the Page* become your steadfast companion as Karisa shares the comfort she's received in her own grief following the suicide of her son. Her walk toward hope will inspire you to not only survive your grief but to trust God through it.

—Linda Evans Shepherd
speaker and bestselling author of 38 books, including *Praying Through Troubled Times*

Turn the Page is hopeful, helpful, raw, and real. Everyone should keep this book on hand in stacks to give to friends in pain who need to hear God. Will. Heal.

—Pam Farrel
author of 60 books, including award-winning *Discovering Hope in the Psalms: A Creative Bible Study Experience* and *Men Are Like Waffles, Women Are Like Spaghetti*

Gripping and evoking. This devotional had my heart on day one. With tears streaming down this grieving mama's face, I was invited into Karisa Moore's tragic pain, a pain no mother should have to endure. But she did, and because I entered the pain with her, I was also invited to experience the hope and healing she found through her Savior, Jesus Christ. Worship has been necessary as I've navigated through adversity, so what a blessing to have recommendations of songs to let resonate each day. Moore's transparency, intertwined with the promises of God, is a healing balm for any reader who has experienced a death loss. It is also a compassionate equipping for those supporting others in grief. I heartily recommend *Turn the Page: Devotions to Help the Griever Hope*. It is a book I wish I had had when my daughter went to heaven, and it's one to keep close and turn to years later.

—Victoria Chapin
speaker, chaplain, author, and director of The Well
Conference for Creatives

Turn the Page: Devotions to Help the Griever Hope

Karisa Moore

TURN
THE
PAGE

DEVOTIONS TO HELP THE
GRIEVER HOPE

By Karisa Moore

FOREWORD BY
DR. MICHELLE BENGTSON

Contents

Dedication

To my Savior—I couldn't' have walked this grief path without the foundation you lay in me as a twenty-year-old new believer. You equipped me with scripture, friends, worship, and motivation to share my story of hope. I love our hikes in nature together. You are constantly revealing to me all the ways that you bring life out of death. Thank you.

To Brian—Held. You cradled me as I wept, lifted my spirits, challenged me when I was stuck in despair, and protected me when the enemy attacked. I love turning each page with you, finding laughter, healing, developing closeness in grief, creating new memories, and celebrating life together. Thank you for holding tight through so many storms.

To Daniel and Natalie—You were so little when your brother died. Your empathy for classmates and adults who have experienced tragic loss is remarkable. Oh, the delight of so many intentional adventures with you both. You remind me not to take myself so seriously, to have faith like a child, and to explore my world with expectation for good things. You are almost grown, and I love watching you embrace all God has in store for you.

To my Word Weavers family—This book blossomed under your critiques, prayers, and support. Thank you.

Foreword

In a world that often dictates how we should grieve and for how long, it can be difficult to find a glimmer of hope amidst the darkness of loss and pain. For those who have experienced the heartbreak of losing a loved one, whether through death or other forms of separation, the journey of grief can seem overwhelming, leaving one feeling trapped in an endless cycle of sadness and despair.

In the depths of grief, it can feel as though the world has come crashing down around us. The pain is unbearable, the sorrow suffocating, and the journey seems endless. Yet, amid our deepest despair, God whispers words of hope, bringing comfort and healing to our broken hearts. As a Christian neuropsychologist and author, I have witnessed firsthand the devastating impact that loss can have on an individual's emotional and mental well-being. The journey of grief is not just an emotional one; it also affects us on an intellectual, physical, and spiritual level.

In *Turn the Page: Devotions to Help the Griever Hope*, Karisa invites us to embark on a transformative journey toward healing, restoration, and renewed hope. Drawing from her own experiences of profound loss and her unwavering faith in God's goodness, Karisa offers a lifeline to those navigating the complexities of grief. Each devotion in this collection is thoughtfully crafted, allowing the reader to enter into a sacred space where they can exhale their pain and inhale the hope that is found in Christ.

With vulnerability and authenticity, Karisa offers gentle guidance and gentle nudges toward healing. Whether you are grappling with shock and denial, anger and guilt, or eventually finding acceptance and hope, each devotion carries a tender reminder that healing is possible and hope can be restored.

Professionally and personally, I have witnessed firsthand both the necessity and power of hope in the healing process. Driven by her passion for helping others find solace in their darkest moments, Karisa beautifully weaves together her personal encounters with grief, biblical truths, and practical insights. Her words resonate deeply, providing a guiding light for those who feel lost in the wilderness of despair.

Turn The Page offers daily devotions that gently lead us through the rollercoaster stages of grief, allowing us to confront our pain while empowering us to embrace our new reality. Drawing from the richness of Scripture, Karisa reminds us of God's promises and his unwavering love, even in the midst of our most profound losses.

Karisa's vulnerability and authenticity create a safe space where grievers can find solace and companionship. With her words, she comforts, encourages, and reminds us that we are not alone in our suffering. She shows us that it is possible to find hope even when our hearts are shattered, pointing us toward the ultimate source of comfort and healing: our Heavenly Father.

As someone who has devoted my life to helping others embrace a life of hope and healing, many of my patients have needed this kind of resource. In a world where grief is often pushed aside or hurriedly processed, *Turn the Page* offers a refreshing perspective. It acknowledges the pain, honors the memories, and provides a roadmap to healing that is as unique as the individual who walks through the pages. With grace and wisdom, Karisa shows us that grief is not a sign of weakness but rather a testament to the depth of love we have for those we have lost.

May this book become a treasured companion, offering solace, strength, and hope as you journey through the wilderness of grief. Open its pages and allow God's tender whispers of comfort to penetrate your soul. You are not alone, dear friend. In the hands of our loving Savior, there is healing, restoration, and a future filled with hope.

Dr. Michelle Bengtson

Board-Certified Clinical Neuropsychologist, host of "Your Hope Filled Perspective" podcast, and author of *The Hem of His Garment: Reaching Out to God When Pain Overwhelms*

Introduction

The day after my oldest son's funeral, I had a decision to make. Would I turn the page on my son's suicide? Would I let his death be a part of my story rather than the conclusion? Many of us who lose a loved one stop living. The temptation to give up is constant. Determined to grieve with hope, I began sharing my story with friends on social media, then on my blog, and now, in this book.

Turn the Page is a sixty-day devotional and journal inspired by my first sixty days of grieving the death of my oldest son, Jonathan, to suicide. You can start from the beginning or skip around as needed—grief is rarely linear. By turning these initial raw pages with me, you can find the courage to walk through your grief with understanding and compassion for your journey. There are many examples of healthy grieving and wise counsel when you cannot turn one more page alone.

Our stories may look different, but interwoven in each is a choice to grieve with hope. My grief included anger, insomnia, and overwhelming fear of future loss. Yours may include self-doubt, ruminating on all the minute details of what if, guilt, fear, or depression. Grief will look different for each of us, but God gives a common language of hope to help us move forward through grief.

In the intro to each devotion, I look back on grief from the perspective of one who has been grieving for ten years. The "Turning My Page" section is adapted from my original public journal as I tried to encourage Jonathan's friends and family by grieving with transparency. Here, you will find my thoughts, experiences, and personal study of scripture during the first days of grief.

You'll see Isaiah 61 referenced in three different devotions. They are life verses that constantly remind me that suffering and sorrow are not the end of God's story. May God gift you a core scripture to meditate on (repeatedly bring to mind) when tempted to despair.

The "Turning Your Page" sections include prompts, questions, suggestions, action steps, and prayers to encourage and spur you toward hope as you process your grief.

If you have not lost a child to suicide, there is still wisdom to glean from this book. Grief is grief. It has common experiences, no matter how small or large. Many wanted to know how to comfort my family in the wake of our loss. Comforters, you will learn ways survivors of any profound loss need comfort.

Below are the words I spoke at Jonathan's funeral on July 7, 2014, which became the catalyst for turning my first page:

> Do we stop the story here or turn the page? Whenever a problem seemed too big to work through, I would ask my son this question. We loved to read stories together, and being an English major, I taught him the basics of story structure. For the hero, there is always a dark page. We determine whether to continue reading their story or put the book down because the obstacles they face seem insurmountable.
>
> Jonathan chose to stop the story when he still had many pages left to turn and fill with adventures.

As many of you share your memories, and I share mine, our sorrow is partnered with laughter and celebration of everything Jonathan has been to us. While I wish he were willing to understand and know that kind of celebration in this life, he now knows it instantly with Jesus!

So, do we turn the page or stop the story here? What Jonathan did is horrible and tragic, and our hearts are raw with aching. But it just is! Every second of every day, we choose how we write our story. Circumstances will come, and things will change, but nothing can change how I choose to write my story. Today, I choose to turn the page and find out what happens next. Maybe it will be another day of grieving; perhaps it's a fireworks display or my children's laughter. Maybe it is an embrace from a friend or someone's life saved. Maybe it's anger. Maybe it's joy. I believe that God is bringing life out of death, just as he always has, and I choose to live this adventure, whatever may come. What will you choose?

At the end of the book, you will find a list of grief-related scriptures you can meditate on, encouragement from a few fellow grievers, a resource page for further follow-up, and my contact information. I would love to hear how God is helping you to grieve with hope. I now invite you to Turn Your Page and continue writing your story out of the darkness of profoundly loving, losing, and loving all the more intensely.

Beginning Grief

*... it is my eager expectation and hope that I
will not be at all ashamed, but that with full
courage now as always Christ will be honored
in my body, whether by life or by death.*
Philippians 1:20

I turned the first page on my son's death the day after his funeral, declaring in a whisper that I would not be defeated by grief.

Though my online presence had been minimal, I suddenly found a community of grievers comprised of not only my friends and family but Jonathan's friends as well. Social media became my platform for journaling out loud as I began to share my grieving-with-hope journey.

My brain, caught in the throes of shock, could not process any new information. God had developed a foundation of prayer, scripture, and friendships eighteen years before the crisis of his illness and suicide. Those habits were crucial in grieving with hope. I could not gain ground in my grief, but I held fast to the truth I already knew about my God. I resolved to stay present and be a witness to those observing my grief, no matter what tears or pain might come.

Turning My Page (my online journal)

My heart hurts beyond belief. I try to read scripture, but my mind fails to absorb it. *Lord, a bit of "osmosis" would be good right now.* My goals for the day are going to the gym, having at least one laugh, and sharing this page.

Turning Your Page

Maybe scripture reading is difficult today, or all you can do is cry out in your pain. Take the first breath. Hydrate. Be present in your circumstances. Shock is a gift. Loss of this magnitude is too much for your body to process. Let your mind and body have free space to work according to need and capacity.

List one thing that you physically need right now.

What do you know about the character of God?

Find a few encouraging scriptures, either ones you know or some in this book. Dwell on those verses and repeat them out loud. Write them down. Hold fast to what you already know to be true.

Pray with Me:

Lord, I am in shock. May you be enough for me today.

Amen

Playlist:

"Held" by Natalie Grant

Allowing the Comforter Into Our Grief

*Blessed be the God and Father of our Lord Jesus Christ,
the Father of mercies and God of all comfort, who
comforts us in all our affliction, so that we may be able
to comfort those who are in any affliction, with the
comfort with which we ourselves are comforted by God.
2 Corinthians 1:3-4*

Looking back, now with a fuller picture of the results of grieving with hope, I see how much grief can isolate. Friends weren't sure how to comfort me and, at times, were afraid of the tears they triggered. I wanted to cloak myself in silence and withdraw, but I chose to allow others to comfort me. My decision to receive comfort was not based on feeling, because I didn't always feel comfortable letting others close to my grief. Instead, my decision was firmly grounded in the understanding that I was created for relationships. The connections might have been small at times, but their touch and impact were mighty. I allowed friends and acquaintances to bring me meals, and I maintained a relationship with my counselor. The comfort I received would not have existed if I had withdrawn.

Turning My Page

Today, my husband and I met with my counselor. The office has a therapy dog, who usually acknowledges me when I come in and maybe even walks me into the session and leaves to help her master.

Today, she greeted us, walked in with us, and then jumped up, placing her front paws on me despite being trained not to jump. The curly-haired doodle rested her head on my arm. I rubbed her head, and then she went to my husband as well. When she left the room, we thought that would be it, but she returned and sat beside me as if it was her job today.

My counselor was shocked. The dog had never behaved this way before. I cried and rubbed her head. When she left again, she still behaved as if she was conflicted, as if she knew that we needed her.

Turning Your Page

God will bring comfort in many forms as you grieve. It is essential to recognize and allow others to comfort you. Isolation is the enemy of grieving with hope. Your surrounding support network may not know what to do for you. Let them stumble. Let those giving comfort be in process, and don't push them away. There may be a few friends you must cut ties with because they are toxic to grieving with hope, but most friends reach out to comfort with their unique gifts and perspectives. Be grateful.

What are one or two ways those around you can help or speak life into you?

Establish a relationship with a biblical counselor.

Record at least one way you were comforted today. For example, comfort can come from people, scripture, and nature.

Pray With Me:

Father, may I notice and be open to your daily comfort in all its forms. Thank you for providing what I need.

Amen

Playlist:

"Afraid With You" by Tauren Wells (feat. Tiffany Hudson)

Hiding Under God's Wings Means Trusting His Protection

*He will cover you with his pinions, and
under his wings you will find refuge;
his faithfulness is a shield and buckler.*
Psalm 91:4

The Psalms were incredibly valuable to me in those first days. Though I tried to read other books of the Bible, I could not take in the message; nothing made any sense to me. I was numb. But when my heart settled on reading the psalmists' words, I cried. I screamed. I felt relief. The writers' words echoed my suffering and my longing, giving me permission to lament.

Turning My Page

I read Psalm 91 last night and this morning. I honed in on the imagery of verse four. God protects me like a mother bird. Such comfort! Through the verse, I learned that when a momma bird senses danger, she will draw her chicks under her wings, completely hiding them. I imagined God taking me and completely covering me with his feathers, and I realized two things: When I am in God's shelter, the enemy cannot see or touch me, and I must completely trust God to protect me because I can't see the enemy. No peeking.

Turning Your Page

The temptation to try and fix painful circumstances is ever-present. Trust God. It is okay to hide and allow your heavenly Father to care for you. Crawl into his lap and allow him to love and protect you when you are vulnerable to attack.

Meditate upon Psalm 91. Write down one verse from the chapter that resonated with or comforted you.

What are other images of protection described in the passage?

What is one small way you are trusting or want to trust God to protect you in your grief?

Pray With Me:

Lord, I need you today. Loss is too much! Protect me. Cover my sorrow with your mighty love. Rock me to sleep, hold me tight as the enemy seeks to crush me.

Amen

Playlist:

"Sanctuary" by Abby Robertson

All My Longings Lie Open Before You, Lord

O Lord, all my longing is before you; my sighing is not hidden from you. My heart throbs; my strength fails me, and the light of my eyes—it also has gone from me. My friends and companions stand aloof from my plague, and my nearest kin stand far off.
Psalm 38:9-11

Losing my son opened my eyes to the many scriptural examples of men and women in various stages of grief. Scripture does not leave us guessing how to grieve with hope. As a result of what Christ did, we know that life doesn't end in death. There is so much hope in knowing that the grip of the grave ended with Christ's resurrection. The physical loss of our loved ones is not the end of God's story.

Turning My Page

It sounds to me like David is grieving in Psalm 38. David sustained substantial loss throughout his life. I am so grateful he shared his heartache because, like David, my wounds are wide open. I cannot hide my brokenness.

In his grief, David managed to cry out to God for reprieve three times in twenty-two verses, but each time, he is swallowed up by grief. Grief is messy. Sometimes, all I can do is cry out. Lord, help me. David knew God would answer, and so do I, but all I can see is this overwhelming pain. So, for now, I cry out, Jesus!

Turning Your Page

Suffering is temporary. Part of healing is putting your struggles outside of you and watching God turn your sorrows into beautiful experiences that touch the lives of others. As you practice grieving with hope, you will develop a growing awareness of how you are encouraging others. Hope does not disappoint (Romans 5:5).

Joy emerges from sorrow in the hands of your redeemer.

Identify a passage or a biblical character that speaks to you about grieving.

Cry out, if you can, and ask Jesus to HELP!

Listen and record his response. Do not give up crying out.

Pray With Me:

Thank you, Jesus, for giving me examples of crying out. May I be honest with you and open to your response. Help me to grieve with hope.

Amen

Playlist:

"Cry Out to Jesus" by Third Day

When Grief Turns Out the Lights

Even though I walk through the valley of the shadow of death, I will fear no evil, for you are with me; your rod and your staff, they comfort me.
Psalm 23:4

God has taught me many lessons throughout the grief journey, but none more significant than trusting Him with what I cannot see or understand. To remain in each moment, in the dark, and sometimes in long, drawn-out silence between touches from God was brutal. But, just like the sun remains in the sky hidden by clouds, I know he is there. The place where my human understanding and God's plans clash is where the lushest growth occurs. Trust in the dark is not easy, but we can count on his goodness. He is our light.

Turning My Page

The kids needed a break. Their little minds need an outlet away from the heaviness of grief. So today, we took a spur-of-the-moment trip to a local indoor waterpark today and the lesson produced gives a valuable image for my surviving son and me to hold on to as we walk through the darkness of his brother's death. Daniel is seven and tall enough to ride the tall slides. We tackled the first one on a two-seater inner tube. He then tackled it alone and progressed to the body slides. But he would not go through the two dark, twisting tunnels.

I admit I had no intention of going on those slides, either. I am slightly claustrophobic. I'm unsure what prompted me to go on the dark body slide alone later, but I did. The slide was like the inside of a cavern, but I was already in the darkest place imaginable. I could not see the twists and turns and didn't know how long the ride lasted, but I knew the light would greet me at the end.

Just before leaving, Daniel grabbed the two-seater and decided to ride the dark slide. As soon as we started down, I sensed his fear. "I'm beside you," I soothed. "The light will greet us at the end." Exiting the pool, I told him, "My relationship with God feels like that slide right now. I don't see him, but I hear his voice. I try to stand on the truth of his character."

In the car, the kids asked to listen to their CD. One of the songs was "You Never Let Go." As Daniel listened, he exclaimed, "That is like the dark slide! I couldn't see you, but I knew you were there. I know God is there, and he won't let go of me."

Yes, Daniel. No matter what storm or dark place you experience, God will never let go of you. Our part is to know God is with us. We obtain that knowledge through reading about his character in scripture, praying, and daily practicing walking by faith.

Turning Your Page

Grief is filled with darkness. Our mind, body, and spirit are under the greatest strain they have ever experienced. It is very much a place of dying to self. Triggers will make you feel like you will never be able to function normally again. Relationships can become more strained. Trauma affects memory. You might be losing things, struggling to keep appointments, and letting daily tasks pile up incomplete.

You may experience a constant barrage of questions. How will I pay the bills? Can I even return to work? How will others react to my loss? Will I ever feel secure again? Will I ever be happy again? Dangers and pitfalls abound during the grief process because you may be tempted to try to escape the pain.

God is a shepherd. The sheep were most vulnerable at night when predators could not be seen. Shepherds were always on alert, kept watch at night, fought intruders, and went after sheep when they strayed. They provided rest and led their flock to the best grazing spots. Their rod and staff were both used to correct and protect. God is present in your grief. Rely on what you already know of his character while you can't see that he will bring you through this trauma. He will protect you in the darkness of grief, and you will see light again.

What is an image that describes or represents your grief right now?

Draw a picture or describe in words what you believe hope looks like.

Meditate on Romans 8:25. Write it out in your own words.

Pray With Me:

I don't understand your ways, Lord. Help me to trust your path, even when I walk through the darkness of grief.

Amen

Playlist:

"I Will Trust" by Red Rocks Worship

Mountains Fall, But I Rise in Christ

God is our refuge and strength, a very present help in trouble. Therefore we will not fear though the earth gives way, though the mountains be moved into the heart of the sea . . . Be still, and know that I am God. I will be exalted among the nations, I will be exalted in the earth!
Psalm 46:1-2,10

Stillness sustained my heart, mind, body, and spirit as mountains crumbled and a tsunami of fear and doubts battered my soul. Jesus was with me. Even when my shocked mind couldn't absorb scripture, sitting with Jesus and meditating on the truth found in the Bible helped me stand firm through the storm of grief.

Turning My Page

How can I remain still in grief and know that he is God? The answer lies in the first verses of Psalm 46.

I know that:

- I am a refugee, and God is my only source of strength.

- He is always available in my grief.

- I am not afraid of the circumstances of my son's death.

Even in declaring these three statements, I feel my anxious heart calming.

Turning Your Page

There will be troubles and challenging days in your grieving. Identify specific areas that are crumbling because of your loss. Are you afraid of more trauma or loss? Look for God's faithfulness in scripture, worship, the lives of others, and nature.

Observe nature and record how God provides for creation.

Do a scripture word search on grief. List at least five of God's promises to us while we grieve.

Allow someone to take care of a task around the house that you don't feel up to doing right now.

Pray With Me:

Calm my anxious heart, Lord. My world is crumbling, but you are faithful.

Amen

Playlist:

"Did You Hear the Mountains Tremble" by Delirious
"Be Still" by Hillsong Worship
"Be Still and Know" by Steven Curtis Chapman

Sitting Down When Anxious to Stand

*And behold, I am sending the promise of my
Father upon you. But stay in the city until
you are clothed with power from on high.*
Luke 24:49

Being calm in circumstances that are very anxiety-forming can be difficult in grief. But many bad decisions are made during a crisis. I very much wanted to move out of my home after Jonathan died, but fellow grievers counseled me to remain. Do not make significant decisions in the first year. It took almost a year for the anxiety to subside, but it did, and ten years later, I still reside in the same home.

Turning My Page

It is hard to imagine a world without my son. From scripture, I know that I'm not alone in feeling unsure of what God expects of me next. As I read Luke 24, I recognize the trauma the disciples experienced in watching Jesus leave them again as he ascended into heaven. As good as the resurrection was, it must have been difficult to fathom moving forward without Jesus physically present. What a whirlwind of emotions they must have felt. So, they stared at the sky long after they could no longer see Jesus. They were stuck! It took angels asking what they were looking at for the disciples to be motivated to act.

Yes, but to what action? Jesus said the starting place was to wait. The Greek word kathisate, which is used for waiting, literally means to "sit down" where I am. Okay, that is a little much to handle right now, Lord, in my emotional state. But Jesus' command to his followers was clear. Wait, even while their emotions were stirred up. He commanded them not to leave Jerusalem but to wait for the gift God promised to arrive. The Holy Spirit is called many names throughout scripture. He is called a comforter, advocate, and counselor.

Can I wait to know I will receive comfort, advocacy, and counsel from the Holy Spirit?

Wait while I grieve my child?

Wait for an answer?

Wait for good things to come?

Turning Your Page

Notice how you feel when making decisions. Grief is taxing your body, mind, and spirit. Heightened anxiousness requires engaging discipline; most significant decisions can wait until you are healthier and able to withstand another jolt. Enlist the help of trustworthy friends to remind you, like the messengers of God, that comfort will come as we abide in Jesus.

Make a list of significant decisions that may be looming. Delegate the ones you can, seek counsel on the ones you must make, and wait on most.

Spend time studying the role of the Holy Spirit in your life.

How and in what circumstances is God asking you to wait for the presence of the Holy Spirit before moving forward?

Pray With Me:

You promised that the Holy Spirit would come. He has come, but let me feel his comfort. I confess that I am tired of waiting for direction in my grief. Teach me to go where you send me.

Amen

Playlist:

"Wait on You" by Elevation Worship & Maverick City

Letting Go of Circumstances

Then Jonah prayed to the LORD his God from the
belly of the fish, saying, "I called out to the LORD,
out of my distress, and he answered me; out of the
belly of Sheol I cried, and you heard my voice."
Jonah 2:1-2

I was afraid. When my husband left for work, I begged
him to call when he arrived so I knew he was safe.
Every time the kids were out of my sight, I was a wreck. I
realized quickly that none of us could live controlled by this
understandable but crippling fear. Loosening my grip took
practice. I spoke the truth over my racing thoughts, found
new delights to focus on—like hiking and photography—and
spent time with friends. Embracing new adventures was the
beautiful outcome of letting go of fear.

Turning My Page

I'm thinking about that pivotal moment in
Finding Nemo (Unkrich, 2003) when Dory asks
the fearful Marlin to trust the whale who has just
swallowed them. Marlin asks her how she knows it
will be alright if he lets go. Her response: "I don't."

We often swim through a big ocean of fear and doubt when we lose someone we love, protect, and sacrifice for. But we need to keep swimming.

How do I let go when I don't know what lies ahead? I have already experienced an overwhelming loss, and now I'm afraid of losing my husband and children. I fight against paralyzing fear, just like Marlin. He lost his wife and children and, as a result, determined nothing terrible would ever happen to Nemo, his remaining son. Yet, bad things did happen. There are sharks, mines, and obstacles throughout the ongoing journey. Marlin learned to let go of his fears by the movie's end and received overwhelming love in return. Not to mention a hefty story to tell. So, in letting go of the circumstances I find myself in, whether good or bad, I discover more love for others and can better receive love in return.

Turning Your Page

Fears abound when you lose someone. You don't know what happens next if you let go of controlling the outcome. But God does.

What do you know about God's character? List one or two traits.

In what areas do you struggle with trust?
List one way you can let go.

Find others in your circles who are further along in their grief to encourage you with the pages they have already turned.

Pray With Me:

Creator, I am swimming in an ocean of doubt. You are trustworthy. Help me continue this adventure and discover how deeply you love and provide for me.

Amen

Playlist:

"Better Because of It" by Danny Gokey

Provision in Despair

It is the LORD who goes before you. He
will be with you; he will not leave you or
forsake you. Do not fear or be dismayed.
Deuteronomy 31:8

God proved my knowledge of his nature valid and reliable as I grieved. To this day, I remain in awe of the many ways God went ahead of my path and continues to do so. What seemed impossible in those grinding days of new grief have blossomed into new friendships, stronger bonds, a closeness to God, and a clearer view of heaven. I witnessed God's care for every detail of my life, sorrow, and faith. He marked a path I could navigate—even in grief.

Turning My Page

I now see that God has gone before us even as we have faced every parent's worst nightmare. Before Jonathan died, a friend had introduced me to a cemetery with beautiful ponds and hiking trails. Jonathan and I had continued to walk there as he grew up. Those walks have been my only connection to any cemetery in the area. As we planned the burial, we had no idea the comfort this choice of resting place would be. It turns out that some of our family, being from the area, are buried in this same cemetery. Not only were they buried there, but they were also in the exact lot I desired. A lot that wouldn't have been available to us if we did not already have family buried there. Long before I lost my son, the Almighty prepared comfort.

Lord, you are committed to me, and I can trust you in my darkest hour.

Turning Your Page

Grief makes your world smaller, but God expands it. Record the small and big ways God has provided for you, even in your sorrow. The truth of his provision is a constant reminder that you are not alone. God's plan is a good one, even in hardships.

Can you see God's provision in your grief? Some ways he provides:

- Community and friendship
- Bereavement leave from work
- Just enough strength for today
- Rest when you expected none
- Surprising moments of laughter
- Scriptures on grief
- Music/Worship

Record specific examples from the list or add examples of comfort you have received in your grief.

Who are the friends surrounding you, loving you?

Pray With Me:

Father, may hope remain the beacon that keeps me turning this page and makes me delight in you. Open my eyes to the path you are mapping out through grief.

Amen

Playlist:

"Worship You There" by The Young Escape

Drinking A Cup of Despair to Offer Hope

*Father, if you are willing, remove this cup from
me. Nevertheless, not my will, but yours, be done.
Luke 22:42*

In the first days, the trauma of Jonathan's death took a huge toll on my body. As a result, my heart grew weary, and I was tempted to despair. I wasn't as willing to obey God in my eating habits or temperament. But when I considered Christ's suffering in the garden as he faced taking on the sins of the world, I clung to the truth that God had a purpose, even in my suffering. Jesus' obedience showed me that I can obey, even on my worst day.

Turning My Page

The stress of my son's death is taking a toll on my body, resulting in infection, my back going out, and difficulty sleeping. I cry out, "I'm trying not to be mad at You, and this isn't helping!" God handles anything I dish out at him. My anger, tears, ups and downs, and all emotions are open to him, just like they were to Jesus as he prayed for the cup to pass from him.

My suffering is nothing compared to Christ's in the garden, just before taking the brunt of God's wrath in my place. Jesus was in so much anguish when he said the above words recorded in scripture that he sweat blood. Sweating blood is called Hematridosis, a rare condition where the body is under so much stress that the blood vessels around your sweat glands rupture. Jesus knew he was about to suffer betrayal, trials, false witnesses, flogging, mocking, crucifixion, and death.

Yet, he chose obedience to the will of his Father, no matter how his body felt. I may not know the whole story of God's plan for salvation, but I do know that God has invited me into the garden to pray. "Not my will, but yours be done ."

Turn Your Page

Seeing your life as part of a broader story of God's redemption helps you believe and accept the results you don't yet see in your circumstances. Pay attention to the testimony of others who are also grieving deeply. Where do they place their hope? What strengthens them to withstand the burden of losing someone they love?

Read testimonies of others who chose hope in their despair if you can. Here are a few who have encouraged me.
~ Elizabeth Elliot—Forgiving and choosing to minister to those who murdered her husband
~ Corrie Ten Boom—found hope while imprisoned in a concentration camp during the Holocaust
~ Beth Chapman—Lost a daughter to a tragic accident
~ Nick Vujicic—born with no arms or legs, overcame depression

Look for a spark of hope in your circumstances. What is it right now?

Pray With Me:

Lord, this loss is too much to handle. But you understand my suffering like no one else can. You sweat blood in your obedience. So help me come to the place where I can say, not my will, but yours be done.

Amen

Playlist:

"Your Will Be Done" by CityAlight

Responding Well to Those Who Don't Understand Grief

But in your hearts honor Christ the Lord as holy,
always being prepared to make a defense to anyone
who asks you for a reason for the hope that is in you;
yet do it with gentleness and respect, having a good
conscience, so that, when you are slandered, those who
revile your good behavior in Christ may be put to shame.
1 Peter 3:15-16

I was an emotional mess the second week after the funeral. There were lots of logistics to handle in the aftermath of death that I wasn't ready to deal with yet, but had to. Exhaustion was the norm, and I struggled to stay the course of grieving with hope. Sometimes, people said hurtful things, and the temptation to pull away was palpable. Grace was needed for myself and others. Forgiveness had to be swift and communication gentle. Grieving with hope isn't about perfection, but it is an opportunity to learn all the more deeply how to love God with your whole heart and love your neighbor as yourself.

Turning My Page

Anger is hard to tamp down right now, not at God, but at people. I have overcome a lot of traumas since childhood, and grief has put me on high-alert for emotional injury. I am catching myself replaying those hurts.

In these few days of grieving, I have experienced both arrogance and humility. Some want to share how I should grieve and for how long. Others try to explain why my son died, but they didn't know my son. They're talking about some abstract person. It feels like they want to explain away death. Others want to slap band-aids over my wounds with verses taken out of the hard context of truth.

But those who approach with humility, and they are in the majority, have invited healing. Even as I write this, the anger subsides. I have been surprised and encouraged by so many who have gone through similar circumstances and have chosen to share their heartache with me.

One mom gave an open invitation for me to join her at a suicide support group, and another person shared her loss of a parent and encouraged me not to give up. Visitors to my church sent a card to say how moved they are by what I am going through and that they are praying. Several teens shared how my son had lifted them up when they were in a dark time. Their humility breathes life into me.

Don't abandon me because I am currently difficult to love. Offer hope like you are planting seeds. God WILL cause them to grow, even if you don't currently see the fruit. Consistent faithfulness in grief is what I need. It's what we all need in our circumstances.

Turning Your Page

You will experience people who try to rush you through grief, but you will also encounter people who walk quietly beside you, hold you when you collapse, and even cry with you. Don't let a few struggling to respond compassionately cut you off from receiving comfort. It is okay to redirect those who may not understand what you need. Sometimes, our vulnerability stirs the wounds in another, and your grief is a chance for them to learn to grieve in a healthier way. If they choose to listen, be gracious! If not, it is okay to let them go. They are where they are, and God can soften their hearts in his timing, just as he is you rs.

What responses can you give to people who do not understand grief and pain?

Pray With Me:

Lord, in my grief, keep me humble. Help me not to react to people who say hurtful things. I wrestle with anger. Show me how to respond with love.

.

Amen

Playlist:

"Church Hurt" Matt Hammitt

Turning the Page on Silence

*For everything there is a season, and a time for every
matter under heaven ... a time to tear, and a time
to sew; a time to keep silent, and a time to speak.
Ecclesiastes 3:1, 7*

Some days, there were no words. I opened my hands to God and asked Him to talk to me; instead, he gave me the gift of silence. I turned the page on the unwritten days and realized I was still secure in who he was and who he created me to be.

Turning My Page:

Today is one of the hardest pages to turn because sometimes there is nothing to say. I don't know about you, but I don't like empty pages. Silent in my anguish? No wise words, no insight into the world's problems. And for today, I must be content with God's silence. To stand and rest on what I already know of God's character, love, and plan for my life. God writes my day, even in the aching absence.

Turning Your Page:

There will be days of silence in grief. It is crucial to develop an awareness of God's purpose for silence in mourning and how you currently respond. Often, in God's silence, our emotions swell, the loss and grief are more painful, and you may be tempted to fill the void with temporary escapes. Do you feel agitated? Are you trying to fill the space with sound? Food? Alcohol? People?

The empty silence of your loved one's presence and what feels like God's lack of response to your immediate discomfort can dishearten, but silence is an opportunity to heal. It moves you out of shock and towards feeling again. Think of the agitation you feel like damaged nerve endings coming to life again. It won't feel comfortable, but it is a step in rebalancing your new normal. Feel the deep ache of the empty chair your loved one should occupy, and trust that God is not distant from your tears. We want the pain to go away. It's not meant to. The gap between what you scrap together in your own strength to survive and God's overwhelming provision for you to thrive is never more expansive than in grief. Choosing to embrace the times God seems silent is an opportunity for greater awareness of your total dependency on him. You can no longer easily lean on your own understanding of grief. Silence tends to reveal what you believe about God and your circumstances. In the quiet, God's love for you shows that he is neither daunted by the magnitude of your loss nor the time it takes to heal.

How do you currently respond to your loved one's absence? Do you leave their chair empty? Is their room untouched? What is one thing you miss about your loved one? Write down, or share with someone, a favorite memory.

What lessons does God teach through silence?

Find a garden, park, or favorite sun-filled spot in the house and sit quietly. What do you hear? What hurts the most in your heart? What does the silence reveal that you are holding onto?

Pray With Me:

Lord, I hear your love in silence. You, too, feel the ache of what shouldn't be. Sit with me. Cry with me. Hold me.

Amen

Playlist:

"A Time to Grieve" by Karen England

When Life Has No Do-Overs, Keep Living

For Christ also suffered once for sins, the righteous for the unrighteous, that he might bring us to God, being put to death in the flesh but made alive in the spirit.
1 Peter 3:18

I don't always get this grief journey right. Frankly, that is okay. There is no perfect way to let go, and so I keep pressing forward with hope in Jesus so that when I make mistakes, such as snapping at my children or giving in to bitterness, I stop dwelling on the errors and look for God's possibilities through my mistakes.

Turning My Page:

"I get a mulligan," eight-year-old Jonathan informed me during a putt-putt game. "
What are those," I asked.
"Do-overs," he explained as he proceeded to pick up his ball and take it back to the beginning.

So, what do we do when life doesn't give us do-overs? I don't have a do-over for my son's death. Each moment is ticking away and counting. Honestly, right now, I feel like two people on two very different trajectories. I'm battling depression, but the other part of me is fighting tooth and nail to live life to the fullest. I know that what I do matters. I see it on your faces. I hear it in your voices. Longing. Something good must come from this. We hope and watch for spring to burst forth from this devastating winter.

Which do you think is more remarkable: a person living the same day repeatedly until they get it right or a person beaten down by life who refuses to stay down and creates energy and hope for others from the fragments of their broken experience? I desire light to sparkle through every bit of my brokenness—a stained glass window of hope, love, and endurance—reflects God-given tenacity.

So, no, my dear son, we don't get mulligans in this life. Instead, we become spectacular new creations of hope through our brokenness.

Turning Your Page:

"What ifs" are difficult to stop asking when you lose someone. And maybe you are asking the right question but not thinking about the best outcome. Instead of addressing the what if toward the past, can you direct it toward the future? What if God takes this evil and saves another life? What if my spouse turns to the Lord? The possibilities are endless for God.

What "what ifs" are you asking? Do they have negative or positive outlooks?

How is grief shaping your faith for the better? Are you becoming more compassionate when others experience loss?

Notice and record positive changes in others because you choose to hope through your grief.

Pray With Me:

Open my eyes, Sovereign God, to the positive outcomes of what if rather than the negative fears of things meant for evil.

Amen

Playlist:

"Glory in the Darkest Place" by Sovereign Grace Music

Oaks of Righteousness
Planted in Tears

*To proclaim the year of the LORD's favor,
and the day of vengeance of our God; to comfort
all who mourn; to grant to those who mourn in
Zion— to give them a beautiful headdress instead
of ashes, the oil of gladness instead of mourning,
the garment of praise instead of a faint spirit;
that they may be called oaks of righteousness, the
planting of the LORD, that he may be glorified.*
Isaiah 61:2-3

Vulnerability is not easy for me. In the second year of grieving, I became aware that I was pulling away from my children, and they felt it. We grieved so differently, yet God wanted us to share each other's burdens. It took intentional action to weep in front of them. I sought a hospice counselor who guided us in activities to create new memories while talking about Jonathan and allowing the kids to see me show the emotions I had been hiding. Vulnerability often starts with a moment of awareness.

Two years earlier, while spending time with a group of teens, I was taught that children need to see an adult's grief.

Turning My Page

It is hard to believe that it has been two weeks since the funeral. Spending four days with teenagers, just as vulnerable to despair as my son, was bittersweet. I miss my teenager! Yesterday at church, I noticed that my posture was guarded. I felt tired and vulnerable. The song "Always Be a Child" by Ray Boltz was sung during the service. I sobbed uncontrollably and wanted to bolt from the church. But I was surrounded by teenagers who could learn from my vulnerability.

As the song played in church, I sat with my arms crossed tightly, tears streaming down my cheeks. I heard God's gentle voice. "Open your arms, child, and receive what I offer you." I obeyed. I put my hands out, palms up, and peace washed over me. One young lady watched me closely; I knew she saw the transformation. She had already reached up to catch a tear moments earlier. She witnessed my grief. She witnessed my God-given peace.

As I bring my sorrows before the throne of God, may they all be traded in for the beauty of the Lord! May I become an oak of righteousness put on display for his glory?

Turning Your Page

Are you afraid to show vulnerability as you grieve? In allowing grief to flow naturally, you also allow God to transform your despair into praise. Grieving with hope takes practice. Be patient and kind to yourself. A good biblical counselor can give you a safe place to share your emotions openly. The psalmists are excellent lamenters because they show emotion and ask honest questions of God. They also illustrate the transition from grief to praise.

What is the worst thing that can happen if you grieve openly? Write it down.

What is the best thing that could happen if you grieve openly? Write it down.

Are others observing your grief? Begin recording ways your grieving with hope is encouraging others.

Pray With Me:

I didn't ask for this deep sorrow, but here I am, Lord, in my weakness. Show others your love through my vulnerability.

Amen

Playlist:

"Oaks of Righteousness" by Mishkanim

Dependent Upon God's Love

*For while we were still weak, at the right time Christ
died for the ungodly. For one will scarcely die for a
righteous person—though perhaps for a good person
one would dare even to die— but God shows his love for
us in that while we were still sinners, Christ died for us.*
Romans 5:6-8

While grieving, I visited a horse farm where gentle methods of rehabilitation were used on neglected and abused horses. Patience, forgiveness, consistency, and persistence were all part of the daily routine. The horses learn to trust their handlers completely. Similarly, layers of trauma and loss have often caused me to lash out when I perceive more suffering.

Today, I catch myself reverting to some of the same reactions I had in those early days of grief. My middle son is the same age Jonathan was when his health deteriorated. Fear threatens to take hold, and I notice more fight-or-flight responses. I cannot always help my immediate reaction to situations that make me feel out of control of my children's well-being, but I catch them much more quickly. God gently guides me toward complete trust in him through scripture, friends, my husband, and church. I firmly believe that one day, I'll follow him anywhere he leads (just like Fred, the horse I encountered at the ranch in those early days of grieving).

Turning My Page:

Fred is a 19-year-old, black Tennessee Walking horse rescued six years ago. Everyone told his owner he was a waste of time. The horse was head-shy and hopeless. Patiently, his owner loved the wounded horse and built trust until Fred followed him everywhere like a shadow. I stood in awe of the bond. He is one of the best horses to ride. Fred is a beautiful, majestic illustration of transformative love.

God is using the same healing methods for me. My heart is broken, raw, and very weary. I expect more trauma and am tempted to close off my heart, but I remember how things were just before Jonathan died. He had pulled away from family and friends. I only had snippets of time with him.

On my knees, I prayed for his well-being and chose to love my son as God first loved me. Not perfectly. Only God has parented perfectly. That choice to love my son afforded us some sweet moments, even amid crisis and heartache. I'm so grateful I didn't close my heart off then. Oh Lord, help me to trust you as I grieve.

Turning Your Page:

Grief may trigger old wounds and reactions for you, just as it did for Fred. Remember the gift of your salvation. Dwell on God's promises throughout scripture that he will consistently walk with you. Lean into the experiences you've already had with God's fulfilled promises.

Even in grief, offer hope through transparency in your vulnerability. Hold on for one more day. Waiting for God in pain. Many in your circle of influence will ask, 'How are you doing this?' You know the temptation of despair. Choosing to love passionately is astounding and touches those around you in their suffering. God didn't wait for us to have it all figured out. So please don't wait until you no longer grieve. Love now with patient, consistent, faithful love, just as you also receive God's patient, consistent, steadfast love.

Why is it important to show love amid grief?

Contemplate your experience with steadfast love from another person and God. What qualities does a steadfast person have?

List one or two people you can encourage this week. What is God showing you about himself or your own character?

Pray With Me:

Lord, I feel the walls closing in. Expand my heart so that I may see grief as an opportunity to love others more deeply and with compassion because I understand their pain.

Amen

Playlist:

"Stay Here (Live)" by The Belonging Co & Merideth Andrews

Patience in Suffering

*Why did I not die at birth, come out from
the womb and expire?" "I am not at ease, nor
am I quiet; I have no rest, but trouble comes."*
Job 3:11, 26

I struggle with Job and other bearers of great suffering. Why would God allow Satan to test Job? He even goes so far as to point Job out. It feels like the God of the Universe has pointed me out for Satan's "special" attention. Satan is looking for me to curse God and die. God is looking for me to trust him and grieve with hope. He is the creator of the universe. I have to accept God laid the foundations and doesn't have to explain himself. He loves me no matter what I experience in this life.

Turning My Page:

I am living with multi-layered suffering. I want to know what patience and suffering have to do with each other.

Patience: from the Latin word patiencia and "endurance," from pati- "to suffer."

•The quality of being patient, as the bearing of provocation, annoyance, misfortune, or pain, without complaint, loss of temper, irritation, or the like.

Alright, suffering is in the very essence of patience and God doesn't always tell us why we suffer, but he did not spare his own son, who was without blemish, and look at the results of Jesus' suffering on the cross. Many were saved.

To truly love others, patience must be my first response to suffering. 1 Corinthians 13:4 says love is patient. "Without patience, love doesn't stand a chance. Patience, at its core, means I am giving up my right to have my way. I am "bearing provocation, annoyance, misfortune or pain, without complaint, loss of temper, irritation or the like."

Barbara Johnson, one of my all-time favorite humorists, said, "Patience is the ability to idle your motor when you feel like stripping your gears." Today, I practice idling my motor and accept God's will for my life. The result is, God ALWAYS brings life out of death, just as Jesus showed in his death and resurrection. Our suffering produces good things when we obey the will of God.

Turning Your Page:

The world is full of thoughts and opinions about suffering. Security comes when we understand God's perspective on suffering. When you're ready, read the book of Job. It is an incredible example of lamenting well, acknowledging God's sovereignty over all circumstances and remembering that he is worthy of praise—even when we don't understand the why behind the suffering.

What is your honest perspective on suffering?

Find at least three scriptures that talk about Jesus and suffering.

Look for and record at least two positives God is bringing out of your trials.

Pray With Me:

I don't want to translate suffering in any other way but yours, Father. So please help me to dwell on how temporary suffering is compared to the glory You will reveal in the fullness of trusting You.

Amen

Playlist:

"Son of Suffering (Live)" by David Funk (feat. Matt Redman)

Resources When Weak

*Then Jesus was led up by the Spirit into the wilderness
to be tempted by the devil. And after fasting forty
days and forty nights, he was hungry. And the tempter
came and said to him, "If you are the Son of God,
command these stones to become loaves of bread."*
Matthew 4:1-3

I develop stronger spiritual muscles in my physical weakness. Though grief taxed every aspect of my body, I now cry out to God more quickly, am open to accountability, and course-correct when neglecting daily habits. Scripture is my sword when the enemy comes at me, and I don't let negative thoughts and emotions make decisions for me.

Turning My Page

Today was rough. I miss Jonathan so much, and my heart hurts. I am physically ill, and I don't have the energy to put up much of a fight.

Jesus was physically weak when the tempter came. Satan went after Jesus:

Identity (IF "you are the Son of God" vs. 3)

Need (Jesus was hungry, Satan tempted him to make bread vs 1-3)

Power (show your might vs 5-6)

Source (worship me, not God vs 8-10)

The enemy attacks the griever in the same way. Jesus knew whose he was, the truth about God's character, and that Satan was tempting him to walk away from his trustworthy power source. My resources:

•Scripture (His established truth)

•God's character (where my identity comes from)

•Power (comes out of focused, intentional worship)

•Authority (Satan must flee when we know who we belong to!)

I hope to get stronger and stronger every day. But, today, I needed the scriptural reminder of Matthew 4—I use the same weapon of scripture Jesus used against the devil.

Turning Your Page

Lay your scriptural weapons on the table. Satan always attacks the same areas: Identity, Needs, Power, and Source. You will be at your strongest when you can recognize these attacks and stand in truth. Jesus possessed the primary education of the Torah that other Jewish boys received. Yet, as early as thirteen, it is recorded that he spent time in the temple long after others had left (a scary lesson for his parents). Even as a child, Jesus understood that his power came from his relationship with his Heavenly Father. You have the same access. Your power to grieve with hope comes from knowing the trustworthiness of a God who loves you. If you feel far from Jesus, keep walking towards him. I encourage you to find your identity in him with a simple heart's cry, "I need you. I want to know you are close." He will answer.

It can help to speak out loud what hurts the most right now. Where is the enemy attacking? Are you snapping more at others? Are you struggling with eating too much or too little? Do dark thoughts plague you?

Pick a few verses to start speaking when your mind, body, and spirit are attacked.

Meditate on Romans 8:28-31 which talks about being convinced that nothing will separate you from the love of God.

Pray With Me:

Oh, Father, I am weakened by grief. Help me to know and rely on the truth of your character so that I can stand against the devil's schemes.

Amen

Playlist:

"Who You Say I Am" by Hillsong Worship

One or Two Lumps of Tradition

Let us hold fast the confession of our hope without wavering, for he who promised is faithful. And let us consider how to stir up one another to love and good works, not neglecting to meet together, as is the habit of some, but encouraging one another, and all the more as you see the Day drawing near.
Hebrews 10:24-25

G rief is never experienced in a vacuum. I had two young children also grieving. We kept some of the normal routines after Jonathan's death. My husband and I saw that if we didn't, any future family events would always be overshadowed by our son's death. The kids took swimming lessons. We went to ballgames and fireworks. We had tea parties. My husband and I celebrated our anniversary. These were, and still are, treasured traditions. My daughter now hosts tea parties for her friends and has the gift of hospitality. We allowed ourselves to experience joy and pain at the same time. It is possible to remember our loved ones while still living life forward.

Turning My Page

My daughter Natalie's birthday is soon, and my mom has a tradition of taking us to a tea house somewhere in the tri-state area each year. We dress up, have tea and sandwiches, and find a new teacup for Natalie's collection.

Jesus was no stranger to a good party. While I realize our loss is going to shake up some of these traditions, it has been important to my husband and me that we press through our heartache to keep some that are special to the kids and us. This tea party would be easy to dismiss, but Natalie has been looking forward to it. So, I choose to keep the date. I know that while this one may be hard, it is still good.

Traditions are essential for my children. Cool things tend to happen in those intentional moments with family. One of Jonathan's favorite traditions was pancakes on Thursday morning after delivering the newspaper with his stepdad. It was four years of bonding, learning work ethic, laughing, sharing stories, and doughy pancakes for Jonathan and me.

Turning Your Page

If you have children or regular events you have done year after year, realize that some of those traditions may not be as enjoyable. Especially right now as you grieve. Some traditions will change. New ones will be established. But both you and your family need to know that not all things will change because of loss. If things need to change, be intentional in those changes. If you need to push through an upcoming event, remember that God doesn't waste a single moment of your grief.

Consider something your loved one enjoyed doing with you and think of a way you can remember them forward. (Remembering forward means doing something new in the present, by yourself, with family, or with friends, while celebrating something special or connecting with your loved one's memory in a meaningful way.) Some meaningful traditions could be planting a tree and decorating it each year at special events, taking a yearly hike, or playing their favorite song on their birthday. Creating a new tradition doesn't have to be something huge.

What is a favorite tradition you had before your loved one passed? Is there a small change that will make it meaningful in the present?

Plan regular times to laugh together and create new memories.

What yearly tradition can you start to help your children honor their loved ones?

Pray With Me:

Lord, I am stretching my spiritual muscles in grief, and new habits are forming in my family. Help us hold on to the traditions that connect us with your love and establish new traditions that transform our loss into the sweetest gains.

Amen

Playlist:

"Jesus Promised Me a Home Over There" by Jennifer Hudson

Setting Our Mind on New Memories

I appeal to you therefore, brothers, by the mercies of God, to present your bodies as a living sacrifice, holy and acceptable to God, which is your spiritual worship. Do not be conformed to this world, but be transformed by the renewal of your mind, that by testing you may discern what is the will of God, what is good and acceptable and perfect.
Romans 12:1-2

I encountered many places Jonathan should occupy. When his friends graduated from college, I placed banners under the tree planted in honor of my son, but there was no graduation party. He has missed out on watching his siblings grow up. His sister has no memory of him. I know Jonathan would have made such a difference in any life he touched. He had a way of noticing when others were hurting. What a joy it would have been to witness him fall in love and marry. I might have already become a grandma. In those days of firsts, I noticed and missed the moments yet to come terribly, but realized I still had to live. So, in areas my son should occupy, I began celebrating differently. I started encouraging others through writing, making sure that I saw people and that they knew I saw them as valuable individuals.

Turning My Page

My heart sank as I looked at the calendar yesterday. I was supposed to be at college orientation with Jonathan this week. The memories I have of Jonathan are lovely treasures, but what do I do with the new memories we are supposed to make? God answered in a spectacular way.

My doorbell rang last night, and it was my neighbors, with two gifts and lots of laughter. They gave me a necklace in memory of Jonathan, and their daughter, who helps with the incoming freshmen camp, brought his college t-shirt. Joy began to fill the cracks of those awful, empty memories as we intentionally replaced them with new moments of laughter, new thought patterns, and healthy relationships. The sadness I felt this week lifted, and I giggle even as I write this. My mind is renewed.

Turning Your Page

There will be new events your loved one should participate in. It is easy for thoughts to spiral down into what isn't. Preparing your heart and mind with intentional new plans is essential.

Why is it important to cultivate new memories?

What are some upcoming events or anniversaries your loved one would have celebrated?

Plan one or two things to do in their honor, get together with friends, and create a new memory.

Pray With Me:

Lord, I can't help these moments when what should have been overlaps what is. Thank you for the refreshment of friends and new memories to soften the blow of what I have lost.

Amen

Playlist:

"Blessings" by Laura Story

The Sweetest Revenge in Grief

*If possible, so far as it depends on you, live
peaceably with all. Beloved, never avenge yourselves,
but leave it to the wrath of God, for it is written,
"Vengeance is mine, I will repay," says the Lord. To
the contrary, "if your enemy is hungry, feed him; if
he is thirsty, give him something to drink; for by
so doing you will heap burning coals on his head."*
Romans 12:18-21

I n those first months of grief, I caught my thoughts stewing, stirring, and playing back horrid scenes. I had to place them under the authority of God. I had no good dreams of Jonathan. Only nightmares. On my knees, burying my face in the carpet, I prayed for and asked God to forgive those who wronged Jonathan. "Lord, rip this anger from my soul!" I screamed. There were layers upon layers of trauma here, and letting go of my "right" to get back at those who harmed my son felt like having my flesh literally torn away. Everything in my soul screamed for justice. I thought about suing. But what would that solve? What relief or resolution would that bring to my family? When I followed the path of anger, hatred, and vengeance to its natural end, I could see that there was no end to rage. It consumes everything in its path and is the enemy of peace and grieving with hope. Some years later, I was able to talk to some of those who hurt Jonathan, forgive them face to face, and see how much his death changed their lives. Surrendering anger isn't easy. Nevertheless, I do not regret the freedom of anticipating good outcomes from God in circumstances Satan meant for evil.

Turning My Page

Revenge will not satisfy the loss of my son. And I want to gain satisfaction. People hurt my son profoundly, and I wrestle with anger toward them. The world celebrates bad guys getting what's coming to them in television shows like *Revenge*, but who draws the line on who is truly evil and beyond redemption? We all have a payment coming to us because we are sinners—death. "For the wages of sin is death" (Romans 6:23a). The world encourages an eye for an eye mentality, but God encourages forgiveness and grace. I am just a sinner judging another sinner when I want revenge.

My response is to respond as Jesus did from the cross. I am to love my enemies and provide for their needs, just as God has extended grace and sustained me. Romans 6:23 goes on to say, "But the free gift of God is eternal life in Christ Jesus our Lord." Witnessing life emerge out of my son's death will satisfy me. That kind of love requires forgiveness and trusting God's will, even in the lives of those who did evil to my son. Mercy is far sweeter than revenge.

Turning Your Page

Have you lost a loved one at the hands of another? Or do you feel responsible? You may feel a whole lot of anger mixed in with your grief. Don't stuff it. Acknowledge how deeply this wound hurt. God acknowledges our anger at being wronged and spells out the best response.

Meditate on Romans 12:18-21. What challenges you? Who handles revenge best?

Write out a one to two-sentence prayer for those you feel anger against.

Take your thoughts captive when you begin to dwell on revenge. Find a safe friend with whom to share this burden.

Pray With Me:

Lord, you alone are entirely correct in your judgment. I will never judge with your salvation for the world in mind. Therefore, take my bitter thoughts and bend them to your great purpose.

Amen

Playlist:

"Forgiveness" by Matthew West

Emotions: Frozen nor Mushy

*Then Joseph could not control himself before all
those who stood by him. He cried, 'Make everyone
go out from me.' So no one stayed with him
when Joseph made himself known to his brothers.*
Genesis 45:1

G rief is emotional. I didn't waste too much time fighting
my emotions because a friend told me from the start,
"It just is." There is no way around the monster of grief but
to grieve. I'm not as triggered by circumstances right now,
but that doesn't mean I won't be for both simple and complex
situations in the future. I am grateful for emotions because
they bring me to Christ for healing.

Turning My Page

Many ask how I am holding it together right now.
The answer is, I'm not.

The key is to let it go—let go of control of my life.
If you have children, you probably just broke out
in Elsa's theme song from *Frozen*. My kids have
been singing this song almost daily.

God created my emotions. They are the outward expression of my state of being. They are not to be controlled, stuffed down, ignored, or used to lash out at others. Instead, I listen to them and adjust my body, mind, or soul's direction. Otherwise, like Elsa, my emotions turn into snow monsters to ward off perceived attacks, or, like Anna, they become fantasies of a different, easier life where she feels loved. Both characters' emotions were out of control because they bought into lies:

Elsa—I must stuff my feelings to be loved.

Anna—I am not loved unless I feel loved.

Emotions are just as much a part of us as our bloodstream, heartbeat, and mind. When our feelings are wonky, so is our body. Emotions express our body's needs, what our mind is stuck on, and the state of our soul. It was not until Elsa stopped holding all her emotions inside and put the storms outside of herself that healing could begin to thaw her frozen heart. It was not until Anna had her heart wounded that she understood her sister and loved her whether she felt Elsa's love in return or not.

I have spent most of my life either being run by emotions or trying to bury them deep inside so I won't get hurt. In the last two years, I have grown more balanced—and not been tossed to and fro by circumstances. My emotions are neither hidden like Elsa's nor controlling my actions like Anna's. I know what I believe, and I know I am God's precious daughter. I am not walking on water but have gotten out of the boat. I am keeping my eyes fixed on Jesus.

Turning Your Page

Think of emotions as your check engine light. Ignore them, and the problem remains. Knots form in your stomach when you try to stuff sobs, and sleep suffers during deep sorrow. God created your emotions to stir you to draw closer to him. Allow feelings to remain tools to guide you toward truth.

What emotion are you currently feeling as you grieve?

What people or things stir your emotions? What can you learn from those emotions?

Read through Psalms 6, 10, and 31. How did the psalmist work through their emotions?

Pray With Me:

Teach me, Father, to be in a right relationship with you through my emotions. Help me not to hurt others but to be honest with my feelings.

Amen

Playlist:

"Weep With Me" by Rend Collective

Death Can't Separate Us from Love

*For I am sure that neither death nor life, nor
angels nor rulers, nor things present nor things to
come, nor powers, nor height nor depth, nor anything
else in all creation, will be able to separate us
from the love of God in Christ Jesus our Lord.*
Romans 8:38-39

L ove wasn't snuffed out when my son died; it exists no matter the losses I experience in this life because God is love. He convinced me of his great compassion for me the moment he saved me. Some told me after Jonathan died that I had a husband and two more kids to live for. But life is fragile, and I recognize that I could lose them, too. I continue to love because Christ first loved me. Even if the worst outcome happens, God is still love, and nothing hinders his ability to love us; therefore, loss does not hinder our ability to love others.

Turning My Page

God did not spare his own son for me. This truth has a whole new depth after losing my son. Knowing I will see Jonathan again in heaven does not satisfy me. God's unbreakable love is what helps me to grieve with hope. I know the demonic forces at work in despair, my sinfulness, and the pain caused by others will not shake Jesus' decision on the cross to love and forgive me.

Turning Your Page

You may not have enough experiences of God's faithfulness to declare that nothing can separate you from God. Yet. God fills scripture with his love and devotion during seasons of loss and trials. By reading those stories and observing the testimony of others, you develop the head knowledge of God's love. Still, you must take the first steps of trusting God's love no matter what happens in this life to experience security in his love.

What does God say about his love for mankind in John 3:16-18? List other scriptures that speak about God's love for you.

Are you convinced of God's love for you? Are there ways your loss is tripping up trusting God?

How does God's unconditional love help you to grieve well?

Pray With Me:

Don't let me live as if my loss separates me from you. You are with me, though my mountains have crumbled.

Amen

Playlist:

"Nothing Can Separate" (feat. Matt Redman) by Lucy Grimble

Woven Together in Hope

*And though a man might prevail against
one who is alone, two will withstand
him—a threefold cord is not quickly broken.
Ecclesiastes 4:12*

M ankind was created as a three-cord strand from the beginning, God and mankind woven together through creation. Friends are vital in grief. I cannot keep putting one foot in front of the other without friends as a part of my three-cord strand. We strengthen each other, speak truth over darkness, and hold each other up when we falter. Attempting to walk through grief alone is a recipe for disaster.

Turning My Page

When I met Jesus, I didn't know how to be a good friend. I was scared to trust anyone and tended to sabotage relationships to keep myself safe. But the day I found out Jonathan was gone, those who loved Jonathan filled my home within an hour. I am grateful God convinced me, long before this crisis, that I was safest and more durable in relationships with other growing believers. As a result, I do not grieve alone or rely only on my thoughts, opinions, and direction. Instead, the community challenges and fine-tunes my beliefs.

Jesus set the example by picking out twelve disciples. Not just for their training and benefit, he needed their support and called them his friends. Then, in his darkest hour, he pleaded with them to stay awake and pray because he felt weakened by what he was about to face.

Relationships are messy, and there is potential for hurt. Jesus was betrayed by one of the twelve and abandoned by the rest. But what a powerhouse they became after the resurrection because they were friends with Jesus and each other. I know I am stronger for having you as a part of my life and a part of my journey. You are a part of my three-cord strand.

Turning Your Page

Lions seek out the weak in the herd, and scripture describes Satan as a lion seeking his prey (1 Peter 5:8). Don't let the enemy of your soul deceive you. No matter how horrendous your previous relationships might have been, you were created for relationships. Friends help carry the weight of grief.

List three friends who speak life into you. What characteristics do they have in common? What gifts do they bring to your grief?

Set up an appointment with a biblical counselor who will lead you to scripture.

Describe your church family. How has worship kept you connected to God? Do they speak truth from scripture over your circumstances?

Pray With Me:

Jesus, friendship is such a gift in grief. Help me to continue to value and be encouraged by friends coming alongside me. Help me to embrace their love and tears with thankfulness.

Amen

Playlist:

"Prayer for a Friend" by Casting Crowns

Finding the Diamond in Trust

*You keep him in perfect peace whose mind
is stayed on you, because he trusts in you.*
Isaiah 26:3

M ind weary. Death's blow depleted my thoughts, spirit, and ability to rest. I forgot things quickly, but the scriptures I memorized in college remained rocks of truth to cling to as the waves of trouble crashed. God established a history of faithfulness in my life, and I repeated those stories. Isaiah 26:3 became a bedtime verse I repeated aloud until my mind stopped racing and trying to control everything. Trust means to be firm, unwavering in purpose, loyal, and resolved. God gave me many opportunities to practice trust, and he proved himself faithful in a spectacular fashion—nothing I experienced was beyond his reach.

Turning My Page

My diamond fell out of my wedding ring.

I panicked. I was in a season of tuning my heart to God's voice, yet my first reaction was to meltdown and panic. Then I remembered that he cares about the smallest detail of our lives.

I lifted my hands to heaven, laid my ring at his feet, and stated, "I trust you, Lord. If you choose to give the diamond back to me, I trust you. And if you don't, I know you have a purpose in that as well."

Peace flooded my soul, and I immediately heard God speaking into my spirit. He gave me precise directions on places to look, but I did not find the diamond. Repeatedly, I praised him and regularly submitted to his will. Every time I prayed, God's response was. "I am going to give you your diamond."

I led a Beth Moore study called *The Inheritance* and set up the room earlier in the day. After an hour of hands and knees searching, I decided to stop looking for my diamond at dinner and focus on visiting with the ladies at my table.

When I went to the Bible study room, I plopped my bags down in a chair, and a glimmer caught my eye. My diamond was sitting on my table as if someone had placed it there for me. I ran around the church like a crazy woman, telling everyone that God had found my diamond. I laughed, I cried, and my trust in him was rewarded.

Nothing is wasted. We gain God's perfect peace when we are unwavering in purpose, loyal, and resolved to stay within his will. I am learning to trust God, no matter what I lose, even after the overwhelming loss of my son.

Turning Your Page

Are you wounded and find trust difficult? People will let you down in grief. Are you expecting Jesus to do the same? As you learn to listen to God's voice and filter out the noise that leads you away from his will, remember his voice will never contradict scripture.

List at least three examples of men and women who listened to God and trusted his voice no matter who stood in their way. ~ Note the characteristics they share and how each person followed God's will versus the expectations of others.

What is one step you can take towards trusting God's direction in your life?

List some doubts and fears that get in the way of trusting God. Then, find at least three verses to meditate on that reflect what happens when we trust him.

Pray With Me:

Trust does not come easy, and I am deeply wounded. The more I rest in your character, the more I witness your goodness, and the steady example of others grieving with hope, the more I realize you are worthy of praise.

Amen

Playlist:

"Trust in You" by Lauren Daigle

Love is the Fuel for Hope

Love bears all things, believes all things, hopes all things, endures all things. Love never ends. As for prophecies, they will pass away; as for tongues, they will cease; as for knowledge, it will pass away.
1 Corinthians 13:7-8

I deal with some unlovable people. Nothing thwarts my grieving with hope faster than dwelling on the wrongs done to me. Men and women caused great harm to Jonathan while attempting to hurt me, and I could have taken legal action. Yet, 1 Corinthians 13 tells me what love is, and it's not revenge. Revenge is self-seeking, keeping a record of wrongs, and a waste of time. And then there is the all-encompassing word "all." in that passage. There is no way around love. It was in my face from day one, and I've not regretted laying down anger and praying for my enemies. Not once. I want the love that never fails, and that unconditional love is found in protecting, trusting, hoping, and persevering when enemies strike me down. God's love never fails, not even in grieving a child lost to despair.

Turning My Page

I don't want to be a noisy gong or a clanging cymbal (as mentioned earlier in the chapter), but I also realize I do not yet love like 1 Corinthians 13 either. Instead, I am often selfish, quick-tempered, struggle to forgive, and want the approval of others.

These faults thwart the effectiveness of my grieving because love fuels hope.

As Paul describes in this passage, love is the Greek word "agape." Agape is a selfless concern for the welfare of others, not dependent upon that person's lovableness. Jesus obeyed God's command and loved me from the cross while I still wrestled with sin.

Turning Your Page

Hope isn't an abstract concept. Faithfulness, charity, and, most importantly, love are concrete. Realizing God loves you changes how you love. It becomes easier to grieve with hope when you are secure in the fact that God loves you.

What is your motivation for grieving with hope?

What are things that get in your way?

How can you protect, trust, and persevere through your circumstances?

Pray With Me:

Jesus, I cannot love well in grief until I realize you mourn my suffering. You are not distant from my despair. Thank you for embracing my sorrow with the open arms of your love on the cross.

Amen

Playlist:

"Love Come to Life" by Big Daddy Weave

Exercising Grief

He gives power to the faint, and to him
who has no might he increases strength.
Isaiah 40:29

E xercise, people, and grounding in scripture are non-negotiables when walking in grief. I spiral when I neglect these things. Hikes in nature quiet and still my anxiousness, photography turns me into a little kid, and friends draw me into adventures. God keeps giving me supernatural strength to embrace life to the fullest.

Turning My Page

When I was nineteen, you could often find me on the streets skating my heart out. I loved it. It felt like all my problems were quiet; it was me, the road, and nature, with music in my ears. Rollerblades felt like wings.

So, when someone asks you your shoe size but tells you not to ask any questions, you might end up with a pair of rollerblades. That's what happened to me when my girlfriends pitched in and bought me some to help me with my new health goal because I had mentioned how much I used to love rollerblading. What a thoughtful gift.

I feel so old right now. My circumstances weigh heavy on my mind and body. But God gives me wings through stepping out of despair, strapping on a pair of inline skates, and flying down the street like a teen again (a little more carefully). The secret to the fountain of youth is joy. I place my hope in Jesus. He trades my sorrows for his joy.

Turning Your Page

Enjoyment may shift after losing someone. The things you once loved no longer satisfy, yet you will discover new loves and new satisfactions. With grief comes the opportunity for joy to develop in spectacular ways.

Do you have a place or activity that brings you joy and strengthens you?

Ask God to renew your strength.

Try one new thing this week.

Pray With Me:

Father, I want to curl up and shut the world out. Strengthen me to embrace my new normal and discover what I now enjoy.

Amen

Playlist:

"God of Comfort (Live)" by Tim Hughes

Heart in the Battle

And the LORD turned to [Gideon] and said,
"Go in this might of yours and save Israel
from the hand of Midian; do not I send you?"
Judges 6:14

Hoo-ah is something the army shouts in response to anything they deem worthy. Just completed a difficult drill. Hoo-ah! Executed your mission with excellence? Hoo-ah! It comes from the gut. Developing a "hooah attitude" in grief is not easy. "hoo-ah attitude" in grief is not easy.

Tragedy can, and has, dragged me into the pit before. The difference comes from my developing confidence in God's character and developing habits of aligning myself with what he says that I am through scripture. Jonathan's death knocked me down, but God asked me to grieve with hope, not grieve perfectly. He knew my weaknesses, yet he still chose me to offer hope to others in despair. He is doing the sending. I will not fail, though weak and battle weary.

Turning My Page

God only wants those whose hearts are in the battle. My heart is in the fight against despair and suicide, but I don't feel like a mighty warrior. The spirit of despair in the world seems daunting and Satan too powerful. I am afraid, but God is not.

In the story of Israel's fight against 135,000 Midianite soldiers, God is so sure of victory that he reduces Gideon's fledgling army down to 300 men to fight a nation "thick as locusts" (Judges 7:12). Gideon asked for multiple signs that God would give victory, and God repeatedly reassured Gideon that he would do everything that he promised.

Fear crippled my life for many years, and though God convinced me of his trustworthiness, my son's death complicated matters. Satan fears anyone willing to obey God no matter where he leads. I will obey.

I choose to offer hope in the face of 49,449 suicides each year[1]. It is easy to be afraid and question God in the face of such a strong foe. Yet, God has given me sign after sign, that he is with me. Like the moments when I can laugh while sorrow still grips me. Jesus already won the victory against death, but I must engage in the battle trusting that promise. What is required? That my heart is in the fight. I watch for the enemy and trust God.

Turning Your Page

Taking ground in grief requires facing the enemy, trusting God, and obeying his will. Desperation may cloud your vision for a while. Your heart may falter, but God does not. Remain steadfast in your sorrow like Gideon did in battle, or Christ remained committed in the garden praying (Luke 22: 39-42). Grieving with hope is an exchange of wills.

What are your biggest fears in grief?

Ask God to confirm the direction he wants you to take.

Can you identify who you are fighting and that God is fighting on your behalf?

Pray With Me:

Mighty God, I do not want the enemy to win one more soul to despair because I didn't fight. Grief threatens to consume me, but I know you have so much more to offer the world beyond the grave of my loss.

Amen

Playlist:

"Make a Way" by I AM THEY

Eating Daily Bread in Grief

Give us each day our daily bread.
Luke 11:3a

I had little understanding of what Jesus meant by daily bread before losing Jonathan. I hadn't yet leaned on God fully. Daily bread is not only enough for me these days; some days, it is all I can handle. Sorrow took a toll on my mind, body, and spirit. I've come to look forward to the daily sustenance God gives me because the delight of his presence is enough for me.

Turning My Page

It has been one month since I put my son in the ground and turned the page on his death. It was hard to believe that I could turn one page, let alone a lifetime of pages. Yet, God has given me what I need each day. Writing this open journal was my daily bread when I wasn't sure I could get through. It kept me holding on.

When storms rage the hardest against me, I am tempted to give up. I hunger for peace, starve for the love of others, am desperate for answers, and crave a different life. The only food that I find that sustains me is Jesus.

Throughout Jesus' ministry, he encountered people who were hungry physically, emotionally, and spiritually. The woman at the well came to fill her bucket with water, but Jesus told her he could give her "water that would never run dry." He loved her and wanted her to live life to the fullest (John 4). He wants to fill me up.

Only when I began eating from my Heavenly Father's table was I full. As a young woman, I tried to sustain myself with earthly things but was never satisfied. Feasting on scripture, God's love, sacrifice for my life, grace, and peace gives me what I need each day to turn the page. I am thankful.

Turning Your Page

You are mind, body, and spirit and need to feed each in grief. Consider your health in each area regularly and allow God and your support system to speak life into your soul.

What sustains you in your grief? What are you eating spiritually?

What do you need today?

Begin recording things you are thankful for each day.

Pray With Me:

Immanuel, nothing in this world can satisfy my sorrow. You alone have the power to bring life out of death and give sight to the blind and forgiveness to sinners. May my satisfaction only come from your well.

Amen

Playlist:

"Lord, I Need You" by Matt Maher

Looking Through the Resurrection Lens at Death

And Jesus said to him, "Leave the dead
to bury their own dead. But as for you,
go and proclaim the kingdom of God"
Luke 9:60

Perspective is everything in grief. The times I became stuck in despair, I had taken my eyes off Christ. Grief and loss consumed me, and I lost sight of God's spectacular provision—friends, comfort, and God's tangible presence had no effect. I lost my source of hope.

Turning My Page

Jesus' words in verse 60 to the grieving man seem harsh. To put it bluntly, I first thought, no wonder some suspected Jesus was leading a cult. Why would Jesus tell him not to bury his father? I imagine the man saying to himself, "This is someone I love, with whom I have a lifetime of experiences. What happened to honor my father and mother, Jesus?"

But Jesus has no issue with us honoring our fathers or mothers, any more than he had a problem with me burying my son. At stake is whether I will follow him at all. The twelve disciples dropped everything to follow Jesus! They didn't say, "Jesus, let me finish catching my fish," or "Let me finish collecting these taxes," or "Let me close my medical practice first."

I must let go of certain aspects of burying Jonathan so they don't distract me from following Jesus. Things like anger, control, and knowing the why. He called me to fulfill Isaiah 61:1-2 long before Jonathan's death. I share the reason for my hope and help others become free from despair. I cannot follow in Jesus' footsteps if I bury my heart in the grave with Jonathan.

Turning Your Page

Letting the dead bury the dead is not the same as never honoring or remembering them. Your life will gain strength and power when you view your loved one's death through the lens of the resurrection of Jesus Christ.

Check in. How are you doing on taking your thoughts captive? What "what ifs" do you dwell on?

Notice what stories you repeat about your circumstances or loved ones. Are they life-giving?

As you grieve with hope, what specific tasks have God given you to accomplish?

How can you encourage others with your resurrection lens on death?

Pray With Me:

Master, I know your provision is enough, but I'm struggling to drop everything and follow you. Break the chains of death that I may live beyond the grave and claim your resurrection power.

Amen

Playlist:

"Hymn of Heaven" by United Voice Worship

Building a Sturdy Wall of Trust

*And I looked and arose and said to the nobles and
to the officials and to the rest of the people, "Do
not be afraid of them. Remember the Lord, who is
great and awesome, and fight for your brothers, your
sons, your daughters, your wives, and your homes."*
Nehemiah 4:14

Recognizing when you are afraid is essential because, like it or not, fear increases after losing someone. Fear is an unpleasant sensation of anxiety or apprehension felt in the presence or anticipation of danger. After Jonathan's death, I struggled with the paralyzing thoughts of losing my husband or the other two children. But as I became aware of how fear attacked me, I spoke truth over each lie and asked for reinforcements when I could not fight the rising thoughts on my own. Catching fear in the act and reinforcing the truth of who God is and who he says we are gives us the ability to build a wall of protection. Our wounded souls need time to heal.

Turning My Page

Like Nehemiah, I am attempting to rebuild my life from the devastation of my son's suicide. Nehemiah was a captive. What was once home, Jerusalem, is in shambles, and everything seems lost. Yet, Nehemiah rallied the people to rebuild, faced his captor to ask for resources and permission to build, and faced a barrage of relentless enemies. Fear must have been a constant temptation for Nehemiah and the Israelites. It certainly grips me right now. I am terrified of more loss.

I fear my attempts to offer hope are in vain, that more loss is inevitable, and that I will lose my husband and children. But when I remember God is more powerful than my circumstances, fear does not keep me from fighting for my loved ones and home. Instead, I assess the situation to gain perspective when facing a threat.

Many of you, like me, are facing daunting circumstances. Your families and lives are in ruins. Some of you weep almost daily for what you have lost or fear you will keep losing. My heart aches with you. We face a real enemy who taunts us, says we will never make it, and takes arms against us when we attempt to rebuild our lives.

So, I stand on the rubble of what was and remind you God is great and awesome. I call you to fight for your families and homes against this stronghold of despair. We will see our city rebuilt and the enemy defeated.

Turning Your Page

Read Nehemiah's story in Nehemiah 1-2. He took the following steps to face his fears. Under each, list ways you can do the same in your circumstances.

Nehemiah looked things over. Describe your current circumstances.

Nehemiah stood up. In what ways can you stand up and battle despair?

Nehemiah spoke up. Who will you ask for help today?

Nehemiah remembered God is mighty and awesome. What can you learn from his behavior, even when afraid?

Nehemiah called Israel to fight for their families and homes. List ways to encourage your family, friends, and neighbors.

Pray With Me:

Lord, I survey my circumstances and am unsure how to mend the brokenness of my loved one's death. Renew my spirit, and help me to rally others caught in despair. Rebuild these walls the enemy has torn down.

Amen

Playlist:

"Christ Alone (feat. Kristian Stanfill)" by Passion

Sharing the Burden of Grief

*"Come to me, all who labor and are heavy laden,
and I will give you rest. Take my yoke upon you,
and learn from me, for I am gentle and lowly
in heart, and you will find rest for your souls.
For my yoke is easy, and my burden is light."*
Matthew 11:28-30

What I learned about Jesus' yoke was revolutionary. Christ's yoke doesn't equal chained and burdened. Yes, grieving with hope is hard work, but what relief I experience in knowing I don't carry the burden alone. Ever. Over and over, he has provided people, scriptural food, and his presence to sustain me. As he leads and I follow his ways, I can navigate grief and pull this load because he pulls with me.

Turning My Page

Weariness was evident when I looked in the mirror last night. Jesus' yoke isn't feeling light if defined as my circumstances. But my son's suicide exists whether I acknowledge God or bring my burdens to Him. My painful loss isn't the yoke.

Did you hear that weary soul? Jesus's yoke is not your circumstances! A yoke is a wooden beam commonly used between a pair of oxen or other animals. The harness enables them to pull together on a load when working in teams, and some yokes are fitted to individual animals.

Based on scripture, Jesus' yoke is:

• Scripture (Every day I read it and am better focused; it is my daily bread)

• Working with Jesus (We are partners, and I do not carry Jonathan's death alone)

• Doing his work (A yoke still implies that there is work to be done)

• Prayer (I can reach out to Jesus)

I feel lighter doing his work. Writing this page is restful for me and gives me a focus for each day. My circumstances are oppressive, but I manage to laugh, love, hold others in pain, and have enough for each day. I will keep coming to him.

Turning Your Page

God did not put a loss in your life as his "light" yoke. His yoke is following him and allowing him to guide you through grief. You may want out of your circumstances. Jesus did, too. He did not want to go to the cross, but his joy was to do the will of his Father and bring salvation to the world. Rest in the fact that God does not leave you to wallow in grief any more than he let death have the final say over his son. He does give rest. And he lifts your burden.

What is the most substantial part of the load you carry in grief?

Look for and record ways Jesus is lightening your load. Are there scriptures that give comfort? Has a friend started walking with you and encouraging you?

Spend time asking God what his yoke is and how you are to work with him through the sorrow.

Pray With Me:

Striving on my own is exhausting me. Teach me to rest in your will and your love for me.

Amen

Playlist:

"Rest (Live)" by Kari Jobe

Cultivating Laughter in Grief

*A joyful heart is good medicine, but
a crushed spirit dries up the bones.*
Proverbs 17:22

L aughter is an intentional goal as I grieve. Whether friends send me funny messages or my kids stir laughter, I find humor in grief. Yes, the loss is overwhelming, but God gives me a plethora of resources to pull me out of the pit, so I can discover enjoyment again.

Turning My Page

Several years ago, I used laughter in preparation for my first surgery by reading Barbara Johnson's book, *Laughter from Heaven*. I read the story of a woman experiencing her first mammogram when the technician exclaimed, "The machine is on fire!" The technician ran out of the room to get help, leaving the poor woman's breast still crushed in the machine. I laughed so hard I erupted in a hyena laugh. My nurse came in to see what was going on. I shared the story with her, and she joined me in laughter. Laughter is contagious.

I learned how effective laughter is in grueling circumstances from Barbara. She faced cancer and the loss of her husband and sons by finding humor in her experiences. I engage my enjoyment muscles during the most profound sorrow I know. I would love to hear a funny story or a good, clean joke, from you.

Turning Your Page

There are many pressing thoughts and decisions to process when someone dies. You need laughter. It may be a part of your personality, or you may have to cultivate humor, but everyone who grieves well also recognizes joy. God sends laughter.

Which friends invite laughter into your soul? Set a time to have coffee with them or watch a funny movie.

Read a humorous mystery or find jokes to share with friends.

Record humorous experiences, things your kids said, or things that make you laugh.

Pray With Me:

A God who named Abraham's miracle child, laughter is a God who brings joy into my life in the impossibility of death.

Amen

Playlist:

"Joy of the Lord (feat. Katie Torwault, Mav. City Gospel Choir & Donte Bowe)" by Maverick City Music & Naiomi Raine

Revving Your Engine When Grief Stalls

But Jesus looked at them and said, "With man this
is impossible, but with God all things are possible."
Matthew 19:26

Grief slows everything down when I stop being intentional and I stall out. I have witnessed others wrestling with the same level of loss who remain standing at the graveside of their loved ones years after the loss. I didn't want to grieve this way, but putting the loss on center stage was easy. I struggled with self-care, completing tasks, and having the energy to engage friends. Finally, I picked a few things, such as making my bed, brushing my teeth, and non-negotiable relationships. When others observed the loss was crushing me, they took my hand and helped me forward. I am grateful God motivated me through the heaviness of sorrow. He moved me beyond the "what ifs" to live life to full measure.

Turning My Page

My son Daniel is a motivator. When he was three, his train table broke; months passed, and I had not fixed it. Though repairing the table wasn't at the top of my priority list, it was at the top of Daniel's, and he reminded me regularly. I fixed it because of his persistence, not because of my own.

A month into grieving with hope, I have moments when my flesh wants to cave to grief, and yesterday was one of them. I am so grateful for people like my son. I felt down, but it is hard to remain stuck with Daniel around. Daniel wanted to walk the neighborhood, pick up trash, and invited the neighbor kids to join us. He wasn't doing much picking up, but he made up a song about trash the whole way. He encouraged us, and I smiled in awe of Daniel's sweet spirit, created in the image of God.

Daniel is an example of God's attitude toward my grief. It is easy to wallow in heartache. No one would blame me, but nothing is impossible with God, and I can step out in faith, trusting that what he says will happen. I stop striving to make things happen, and my fear is dispelled once I accept that death cannot thwart God's will.

Turning Your Page

You are in the early days of grief. You may not feel motivated to do very much. Take small steps—keep moving forward. You have an enemy who wants to devour as many of God's creations as possible. Grief can motivate you to embrace all God deems possible or pull you away from Him. Pay attention to the people God places in your path and where he is leading you.

Evaluate what drags you down physically, mentally, and spiritually. What picks up your spirit and motivates you?

Pick five things you will do that are not optional.

Here are some other scriptures with similar wording to Matthew 19:26:
Genesis 18:14 ~1 Samuel 14:6 ~Job 42:2 ~Jeremiah 32:17, 27 ~Luke 1:37

Pray With Me:

Lord, You are at work in me even when I feel weak. Thank you for family and friends who motivate me forward to embrace life beyond the grave.

Amen

Playlist:

"Impossible" by Sidewalk Prophets

God Gives Full Life in Grief

The thief comes only to steal and kill and destroy. I came that they may have life and have it abundantly.
John 10:10

I expect God to bring good things out of my son's death. Years into grieving with hope, I can tell you that others on the brink of suicide have chosen life. Many opportunities have emerged from my loss to offer hope to others burdened with overwhelming loss. I met some of Jonathan's friends for the first time because of his death. They shared how Jonathan's life and even death motivated and changed them. I pray they continue to live life to the fullest. I choose life every day.

Turning My Page

Life has dealt me a difficult hand, and sometimes I wonder why God didn't make us obedient robots without free will. Every day, I hurt. But God isn't distant from my pain. He got up from his throne and chose with his own free will to take on the form of a helpless baby. Jesus understood my suffering and came that I would have life to the fullest. He grew and showed me what happens when I accept God's will over my own.

The devil thought he won when Jesus died on the cross, but on the third day, Jesus turned the page on death and the world has never been the same. I turn the page on Jonathan's suicide by choosing to grieve with hope. My hope is that God will bring life out of my son's death. The devil meant this for evil, but God will use it for good.

Turning Your Page

Keep turning your page. The story God is writing is not over yet. Your life touches so many others, and by turning the page on your loved one's death, you declare to Satan, "You do not get the final say."

Identify ways you are spiritually under attack while grieving. Do others tell you how to grieve? Are the same thoughts repeating? Do you struggle with flashes of finding your loved one in unexpected places?

Biblical counsel is a valuable resource in grief. You may have to wrestle with the mystery of our free will and God's sovereignty. Ask a trustworthy counselor to help with scriptures and questions about God's part in your loss and grief.

Take a stand against the devil by recognizing the ways he attacks and combatting it with the truth of scripture.

Pray With Me:

There is no substitute for your ways, Lord. You are my source of abundant life in grief; the enemy cannot steal it from me.

Amen

Playlist:

"Goodness of God" by Bethel Music &Jenn Johnson

Meeting Joy in Grief

*Therefore, since we are surrounded by so great a cloud
of witnesses, let us also lay aside every weight, and sin
which clings so closely, and let us run with endurance the
race that is set before us, looking to Jesus, the founder
and perfecter of our faith, who for the joy that was
set before him endured the cross, despising the shame,
and is seated at the right hand of the throne of God.*
Hebrews 12:1-2

J ust a few months after Jonathan's death, I attended a
Suicide Prevention Walk. Both painful and joy-filled. The
thoughtfulness of everyone involved made it a memory worth
having. I especially loved the college-age students lined up to
give a hug if we wanted it. Having young men my son's age
hug me was like having my son hug me. I treasure them, and
they also motivated me to think of ways to encourage others
in their grief.

Turning My Page

My family visited a local amusement park yesterday.
We originally planned on visiting the week of
Jonathan's death. I did well and even laughed at
the littles as they zipped from ride to ride. But
the "Jonathan void" overwhelmed me for several
moments. He should be here. I asked my husband if
I would stop feeling the empty space. He shook his

head no. The ache of my loss weighs every shout of j
oy.

Jesus was deeply familiar with sorrow but also pressed into the joy of God's love. I may carry around the heaviness of Jonathan's death, but I also carry the lightness and joy of Jesus' love for me. He came that I might have life to the fullest. I press into living.

Turning Your Page

Joy-infused sorrow may seem impossible, but it remains present where life happens. Engage meaningful activities with friends and family—joy comes no matter the harsh realities of our loss.

Pick an activity and develop a new memory, even if the feelings aren't there yet.

Record a moment when you felt joy, laughed, and enjoyed life. What made the moment special? Who was involved? Did you also feel sadness?

Is there a way you can serve your community? Pick a small step you can take to engage the world around you.

Pray With Me:

Lord, I don't want to feel this heartache. It overwhelms. Help me engage others and create new memories no matter how much I hurt. I am ready to embrace joy.

Amen

Playlist:

"Even If" by Mercy Me

Studying God

And the child grew and became strong, filled with wisdom. And the favor of God was upon him. ... And he said to them, "Why were you looking for me? Did you not know that I must be in my Father's house?"
Luke 2:40,49

I grew up in the church but did not understand the concept of a personal relationship with Jesus. My knowledge of God, Jesus, and the Holy Spirit had little to no effect on me. As a twenty-year-old mother, I met Jesus. I experienced the gift of salvation, so I wanted to know who I am and whose I am. Other believers poured a solid foundation of scripture, prayer, fellowship, and witnessing into my soul, which now sustains me in my darkest hours.

Turning My Page

> My kids must return to school today, and as they do, I realize I am a student, too. God is teaching me to grieve with hope because I have an enemy who knows scripture well enough to twist it. My strength to combat Satan comes from knowing Jesus, obeying his will for my life, and sharing the gospel with others.

Jesus may have been God in the flesh, but he wasn't born with an extensive biblical vocabulary. He didn't get to skip school. His disciples also had no formal training when Jesus called them to minister. They spent three intensive years with Jesus, and I believe they continued studying scripture as they preached the gospel.

I want to learn to love God wholeheartedly, walk in his ways, and do the things that will keep my mind, body, and soul healthy. I study him because knowing Him means I navigate grief with a friend.

Turning Your Page

You may not know much about God, Jesus, or the Holy Spirit yet, but learning about each characteristic of God lightens your burden. He knows you. Knows exactly how you function best and what will bring you comfort. Be strengthened by the one who removed his cloak of royalty to understand your suffering. He loves you.

To hope means to trust or rely on something you don't yet see. Take a walk and meditate on Hebrews 11:1. Contemplate how you can use this scripture to combat an emotional, spiritual, or physical attack.

List some scriptures you want to meditate on. Write them out on a notecard or sticky note. Pull two out each week to meditate on and say out loud.

How is grief revealing God's character?

Pray With Me:

I admit I don't know how to grieve with hope very well. Your ways are not mine. I want to trust you as I suffer. Make me secure in faith as I study your character.

Amen

Playlist:

"He Will Hold Me Fast" by Shane & Shane

Bringing the Stars in the Darkness of Depression

*And they heard the sound of the LORD God walking
in the garden in the cool of the day, and the man and
his wife hid themselves from the presence of the LORD
God among the trees of the garden. But the LORD God
called to the man and said to him, "Where are you?"
And he said, "I heard the sound of you in the garden,
and I was afraid, because I was naked, and I hid myself."
Genesis 3:8-10*

Depression has its origins in the Garden of Eden. Our vision clouds with fear because of the first bite mankind took of the fruit of knowledge of good and evil. Everything instantly looked different to us-our bodies, our circumstances, each other, and even God." A gap formed. Salvation could be inches away, but we do not seek help because we fear God's ways.

This devotion comes with a warning. Very few of us are ready for this level of ministry in the beginning stages of grief. I was not. I was so focused on bringing life out of my son's death and ministering to his friends and family that I forgot that was God's job and not mine. All he asked of me was to abide in him. Even in grief, we can minister in little ways, just by being transparent with others, but trauma of any kind takes time to heal—mind, body, and spirit. Give yourself time to grieve.

Turning My Page

As I studied scripture, I looked for the root of depression. I wanted to know what God said about why suicide exists and why, despite our best efforts, we can't seem to eradicate this destructive enemy. To understand depression, I had to go to the beginning of mankind's story.

My dictionary defines one kind of depression as the "angular distance of a celestial object below the horizon." I believe that definition also visualizes what happens to us internally during depression. We cannot see the events or people that will give us hope, help, and healing over the horizon.

So how can we help friends, family, or acquaintances who are depressed and who stand on one side of the divide while we stand with a clear view of the horizon? We form a bridge by standing in the GAP. We Gather, Assess, and Provide.

By gathering information about our loved one's current circumstances, we can better evaluate their state of mind, body, and spirit. We then can make decisions based on the "intel" gathered. If my friend's depression stems from how she's feeling about her body weight, then I assess that bringing her a large box of chocolates to cheer her up is probably not helpful.

Provision is tricky. When the first signs of depression occur, you are the best person to offer help. You are on the front lines and with the person day in and day out. No doctor or counselor occupies such a strategic position.

Provide hope, help, and healing. These don't require complicated responses—the simple consistency of your presence may be enough. Within an hour of my initial call to the church, family, and friends after Jonathan's death, they filled my home. No one knew what to say, but having them present with us in our shock and grief was enough.

You can provide but not force your loved one to partake in life. Accepting rejection is difficult, but don't let it stop you from continuing to offer. Keep coming over the horizon, bringing a report of the heavens. You provide a chance for vision to clear and for your loved one to know celestial bodies exist beyond, whether they see them or not. You bring them the stars.

Turning Your Page

You may feel overwhelmed by the depression of a loved one. God gives you the tools to remain steadfast in your suffering. You know the emotional toll of despair, the physical drain of loss, and the darkness of a new normal. Use your experience to show others how to stand firm even when the feelings don't match.

Spend some time watching a sunset or sunrise. What do you observe about the changes? How can you find peace in what you currently don't see in grief? (i.e. I don't currently see God working, but I know in the past he has done x, y, z in the past.)

Who in your life needs encouragement?

What steps can you take to familiarize yourself with their struggle with grief?

Pray With Me:

God, I don't understand Your ways, yet I find hope, peace, love, and forgiveness when I trust You. Teach me Your ways so that I may encourage others who need to know they are valued.

Amen

Playlist:

"Everyone Needs a Little" by Kari Jobe

Enjoying the New Normal

*Rejoice in hope, be patient in
tribulation, be constant in prayer.*
Romans 12:12

I didn't expect joy in the first days, yet new delights came. A giggle here, a smile softened my sorrow, and quiet peacefulness emerged during hikes through nature. New memories formed because I intentionally placed myself where joy resided and looked for hope in the cracks of my circumstances. My sweet children sprinkled joy into my life almost daily, and though I bore the deepest heartache, I learned to embrace God's love through their innocence.

Turning My Page

Since Jonathan's death, the kids have wanted to sleep in the loft beds. Last night, their daddy said yes, but he warned them: No talking, it's time for sleep. A few minutes later, I heard them chatting away and giggling profusely. I told them to settle down, but whatever they had to say to each other was more important than obedience.

Joy overwhelmed me as I listened to their happy sounds. Jonathan's death is painful for them, and hearing their usual chatter refreshed me. They eventually settled. Enjoying myself, even in the exhausting journey of grief, is okay. God sent his only son into the world's turmoil to be present with us. I do not believe Jesus was the tortured, melancholy man the way many films portray him. Scripture records many of his more intense moments but also pictures him happy and full of life. I can't imagine him saying, "I've come that you may have life abundantly" (John 10:10) if he was not full of life himself. Finding moments of laughter in the grief process is precious. Enjoy them.

Turning Your Page

Jesus tells his disciples to become like little children. Your grief is an opportunity to explore a childlike faith. You have a new normal, and in this challenging place, you discover new loves, passions, and memories of joy.

How can you play in grief? What discoveries, new loves, and new adventures would you like to have? Record the sweet moments with your family or friends.

Find an art class or take a step to explore an activity you've always wanted to try but never have.

List some specific examples of ways God has surprised you with joy in your grief. If you have not experienced any, look for moments you laughed this week or ways someone encouraged your spirit.

Pray With Me:

Lord of joy, give me hope as I observe your creation and peace through the creation of new memories. Help me recognize your encouragement along the path of grief.

Amen

Playlist:

"Joy in the Morning" by Tauren Wells & Elevation Worship

But Hope Never Fades

*May the God of hope fill you with all joy
and peace in believing, so that by the power
of the Holy Spirit you may abound in hope.
Romans 15:13*

D reams of Jonathan rattle me. They are never pleasant and reveal my feeling of helplessness. I couldn't save him. I must take those thoughts captive and say, "It was never my job to save him; it was yours." The God of the universe knew my son's struggle in intimate detail, and no amount of attempting to be God would change the outcome. I can't do a better job than the one who knew what Jonathan needed.

Turning My Page

Rough turning today's page. Again, a dream about Jonathan. I was close but could never hold him. The heaviness was oppressive as I started my day, but hope came from a funny source. I was headed to meet a friend and heard on the way that Honest Tea did a "National Honesty Index." They displayed their tea in cities in all fifty states and charged a dollar on the honor system. The result was that 95% of all people paid. It gives me hope that so many people chose to be honest when no one was watching them.

Our world is broken, and many stories exist similar to my own. We need hope. When Jesus arrived, the world was desperate for hope. He described himself as the hope and light of the world.

We speak of the word hope all the time—I hope I get the promotion, hope he pulls through, I hope I meet the right man—we lose sight of the depth of its meaning. Hope is the foundation for joy, peace, and trust. Putting my grief in the hands of a loving, compassionate, and just God means I will never be disappointed by hope. I may not be able to hold Jonathan, but I can hold others through God's love! May my obedience be a display of overflowing hope.

Turing Your Page

The feelings of joy, peace, and trust will rise and fall as you grieve but hope never fades. As you grow in faith and understanding, you will accumulate stepping stones of joy, trust, and peace to rely on and return to when you falter. These stepping stones become tangible reminders of God's goodness and how far hope has taken you. Hope is a choice you make to see suffering differently. Rather than a limitation, hope-shaped grief is full of possibility and opportunity.

On a scale of 1 to 10, where would you rank your current joy, peace, and trust?

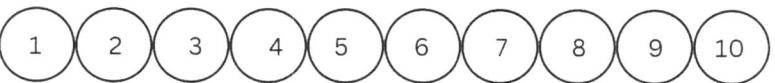

Finish the following statement: I miss _____ so much it hurts, but I hope that God uses my loss to . . .

Find a smooth stone to paint and decorate. Write down a hope you currently have or a hope that has already been fulfilled.

Pray With Me:

Lord, I declare I trust you with my circumstances. Fill me up today with your joy and peace. I anticipate your goodness today.

Amen

Playlist:

"Firm Foundation" by Cody Carnes

Love Notes From God

If you remain in me, and my words remain in you,
ask whatever you wish and it will be given to you.
John 15:7

God has often spoken directly to my grief in unique ways. I call these love notes. Sometimes, his notes of love surprised and delighted me when I wasn't looking for them, such as a bird spending time singing to me on the windowsill. Other times, I watched for them expectantly, and he did not disappoint. God is not distant from my suffering and reminds me that he has a purpose in all I experience.

Turning My Page

God gave me several delightful love notes yesterday. Love notes are anything I tell only God, and he provides what I desire spectacularly. One such desire was to see a woman I met during the first session of swim lessons. I regretted not getting her number, and I was hoping to see her again, and God provided an opportunity. She was at the pool when we arrived for an open swim.

Even with these beautiful love notes, I struggle to believe God will give me the big things I desire. There have been many things that I have asked for that haven't happened. But, even as I wrestle, I am currently teaching my children to take hold of John 15:7.

Daniel took the verse literally and shot back to God, "Okay, I want my brother back!"

I do not exactly know how this verse works, but I agree with Daniel. I want Jonathan back. I explained to my son that God is not a genie forced to give me three wishes. He did not spare his own son. Jesus didn't want to drink the cup of suffering God set before him any more than I do. But the Savior declared, "Not my will, but yours be done." So he remained in the vine of his father.

Remain is "continuing to exist, especially after other similar people or things have ceased to do so" (Oxford Online Dictionary). Wow! Jesus most certainly fulfilled this definition. I must remain in Jesus and boldly ask him what I want. And by remaining, I ask for things that are wholeheartedly within the will of the Heavenly Father.

Turning Your Page

God cuts off any branch that is not bearing fruit and prunes every branch that produces fruit to bear more. The key to bearing much fruit is to remain attached to Jesus. Allow his words to be the nutrition pumping through your veins as you grieve.

Read through John 15
Why would God give us whatever we ask for in grief?

What three habits does Jesus say you must form as a believer to ask and receive from God?

Pray With Me:

Lord, you give me love notes as I grieve. Open my eyes so that I may see you are writing a beautiful story, even when I want { _____*Insert your loved one's name*_____ } back.

Amen

Playlist:

"How Great is Your Love" by Phil Wickham

Using Gifts in Grief

For just as the body is one and has many
members, and all the members of the body,
though many, are one body, so it is with Christ.
1 Corinthians 12:12

Just as Jesus needed his friends in the garden, I needed others to encourage and speak life into me in big and small ways. I do not have all the gifts necessary to grieve well. So many have blessed me with the gift of hospitality. Others have cared for my soul through listening and laughter. Big and little matter to me. I have learned so much about how to use my gifts to help others as they grieve.

Turning My Page

We grieve together, but we must also rejoice together. God created me with a love and passion for writing. This public journal was designed to encourage the body, even as I grieve. The body of Christ has suffered the loss of Jonathan with me. They have mourned, ached with me, and served my family with their spiritual gifts. We have been blessed by meals, encouraging cards, jokes, listening ears, cleaning, and much more. Their passion uplifted my own and encouraged me as I wrote these pages.

The body of Christ is a storehouse of comfort and celebration. We can both hold and challenge one another in breathtaking displays of the Lord's splendor.

Turning Your Page

God created the church, and he placed a specific passion in each of you. Doing your part and not attempting to take over the roles of others in the body of Christ makes you a dynamic and effective griever.

What gift do you gravitate towards? Do you like doing hands-on work or supportive roles?

How could the early church be of one mind when each disciple differed in thinking?

Do you feel resentful of other parts of Christ's body? Develop wonder and awe that God created us differently and yet a part of one spirit.

Take steps to use your gifts to encourage someone as you grieve. Write down one action plan.

Pray With Me:

Creator, how have you uniquely gifted me? I acknowledge that nothing is too small. Help me to grieve well by accepting the good gifts of love others offer and kindle in me love in return.

Amen

Playlist:

"Prayer for a Friend" by Casting Crowns

Extra! Extra! Read All About Grief

Again I saw all the oppressions that are done under the sun. And behold, the tears of the oppressed, and they had no one to comfort them! On the side of their oppressors there was power, and there was no one to comfort them.
Ecclesiastes 4:1

My view of news and movies changed because of Jonathan's death. I feel physically ill when I take in too much of the world's ugliness. I need Christ above all else. His word, truth, and passion for the world are a balm to my deeply wounded soul. Movies with gratuitous violence hurt my head, and my soul's taste buds are no longer dead to evil. I was blind, but now I see.

Turning My Page

The book of Ecclesiastes reads like a modern-day newspaper. It reports man's depravity and asks, "What is the point of living if this is all there is?"

The restaurant where my son worked placed a plaque on the wall in his honor. Going there is hard for me, but my children connect with their brother there, so I go. On a recent visit, some college-age kids were sitting close, and I could hear their conversation. They were making fun of each other and others who attended a recent party. These teens were so drunk that they didn't remember much. My heart broke as they described getting sick, making fools of themselves, and passing out.

I couldn't stand it. Here I was, desperate for a college phone call from my son, and these kids were devaluing and, worse, putting their lives in jeopardy. I pointed out my son to them and encouraged them to live life to the fullest.

Since Jonathan's death, it has been difficult for me to watch TV or hear worldwide news. Yet, I can't get away from the world. I witness oppression, violence, mutilated relationships, and the pointlessness of fighting to be on top—daily. It's in my face and affects me profoundly. It is easy to sink into hopelessness when day in and day out, many of us struggle with our purpose, sin, doubts about God, and loss.

I want to see oppression replaced by generosity towards one another. Jesus came that we may have life and have it abundantly. He broke into our news cycle and gave all mankind a new headline: REDEEMED, THIS PERSON LIVES FOR OTHERS!

Turning Your Page

You may react more strongly to the conversations around you. This is normal. Losing someone is an opportunity to revamp our wrong thinking and see how valuable life is. It will be easy to respond to others with anger. Still, once you understand the root —the grief you feel for your loved one—you can learn to encourage others to live life to the fullest rather than turn to judgment.

What is your reaction when you read the current headlines or hear of the latest political fight?

How has grief changed your perspective on the behaviors of friends, neighbors, and strangers?

How has what you value changed?

List new priorities.

Pray With Me:

Father, I am judging others and reacting more harshly because of my loss and exhaustion. I have no patience for wasted living. Help me recognize where I waste life and teach me to be gracious to others in their process.

Amen

Playlist:

"Even When It Hurts (Praise Song)" by Hillsong United & Taya

Any Last Words

*And Jesus came and said to them, "All authority
in heaven and on earth has been given to me.
Go therefore and make disciples of all nations,
baptizing them in the name of the Father and of
the Son and of the Holy Spirit, teaching them to
observe all that I have commanded you. And behold,
I am with you always, to the end of the age"*
Matthew 28:18-20

I am deeply aware that my time on this earth is short. I want those who cross my path to know they are loved and valued and life on this earth is worth living. Jonathan's death gave me an urgency to share what I have learned about God.

Turning My Page

My last words to Jonathan were, "See you this afternoon." I thought we had more time. I will have a final post one day. What do I want family, friends, enemies, and the world to utilize from my life? In other words, what is my testimony at this very moment, not an abstract future date?

Jesus said in 1 Peter 3:15 that when people ask, I should have an answer for the reason I have hope.

Three things that I would love for you to take from my life:

1. God is faithful. (He keeps his promises)

2. Life is not easy, but peace and joy are available through Jesus Christ.

3. Scripture is a road map and tool to stand against our enemy, Satan.

If these devotions infuse hope into your trials, turmoil, and loss. Pass your confidence on to those who cross your path—this is the best encouragement I can receive.

Turning Your Page

The best testimony is the one that lives on in others. Jesus shared his hope with the disciples and then told the disciples to share that hope with the world. What is your testimony?

What were the last words you said today to your loved ones?

List things you would like your present loved ones to take away from how you lived.

Write your testimony. How is God proving himself faithful, and what is he teaching you through grief? What lessons are you learning about grace and forgiveness?

Pray With Me:

Author of Life, my loved one's death is not the end of my story. Open my eyes to the ways you are helping me to grieve with hope so that I can answer anyone who asks how I keep moving forward.

Amen

Playlist:

"Legacy" by Nichole Nordeman

Setting Goals to Get Out of the Boat

And Peter answered him, "Lord, if it is you, command me to come to you on the water." He said, "Come." So Peter got out of the boat and walked on the water and came to Jesus. But when he saw the wind, he was afraid, and beginning to sink he cried out, "Lord, save me!"
Matthew 14:28-30

Letting my children struggle is an ongoing lesson. Recently, God stepped into my anxious attempts at fixing things for my daughter and told me, "I'm bringing her to me. Stop interfering." Much of my struggle comes from a desire to know things will turn out well for them. God knows better than I do, and I miss out on the joy of my children growing and discovering when I shift to control the outcome.

Turning My Page

It is hard to let my kids sink. Today, I enjoyed swimming with my husband and kids. Daniel has become part fish, and Natalie is close to joining him. Daniel set regular goals for himself and kept going after them throughout the summer. Natalie began doing the same this week. She tossed a toy and tried her hardest to swim to it. At times, she asked me to let her go.

I knew she was in no danger because she was always within reach. But as she stretched out into uncharted waters, I didn't want her to fail. She might become frightened and not try again. But Jesus lets us fail.

Jesus let Peter get out of the boat. He also let Peter sink. Why would a loving God let us sink? God allows us to fail because he wants us to learn to trust him, and he can rescue us.

Peter stepped out further in faith, but by stepping out, he revealed where his doubts still caused him to sink. When Peter returned to the safety of the boat, he and the other disciples worshiped, declaring, " Truly you are the Son of God." They learned more about God and themselves in that moment of faith and rescue.

Sometimes, I think I am drowning in my circumstances. I cry out for Jesus to save me, but he doesn't immediately. God is concerned with my long-term faithfulness and implements his plan for salvation. He removes my doubts and strengthens my faith. Even if I don't walk on water this time, like Peter, fear will not have the final say over me.

Peter was the first disciple to testify to who Jesus was after the Resurrection (Acts 2), and tradition holds that he was later crucified for preaching the gospel. He got out of the boat and kept his eyes fixed on Jesus. He walked on water.

Step out of the boat of grief with me.

God has asked me to go into uncharted waters. I told you in a previous post that I'm out of the boat, but the wind has whipped up this week, and I've felt like I was sinking. God is bringing my doubts to the surface and strengthening my faith. Whenever I've cried out, he reaches out and brings me to safety.

Turning Your Page

Getting out of the boat in grief is tense. You've already experienced loss and may struggle to trust that God wants good things for you. But, he does.

What do you think it took for Peter to get out of the boat?

What gets in the way of your trusting God?

Take one faithful step to trust God in grief.

Pray With Me:

My heart is pounding. To trust that you want good things as I grieve is terrifying. The what-ifs cloud my thinking. Help me fix my eyes on you to wow the world with possibility.

Amen

Playlist:

"Walk on The Water" by Britt Nicole

God is Faithful in Doubts

And he said to them, "Why are you troubled,
and why do doubts arise in your hearts?"
Luke 24: 38

God's faithfulness is at the heart of why I remain steadfast. Losing a child is unnatural, and I will always feel Jonathan's absence as a mother. The toll his suicide has taken on my mind, body, and spirit is extensive, but God's impact is greater. I have witnessed others choose life, my family cares more deeply for the suffering, and I have become a resource for those suffering from despair.

Turning My Page

How my husband and I can get up today is beyond me. From a physical standpoint, we are not sleeping. Emotionally, the ache of missing Jonathan has deepened. Questions surfaced. Why didn't others listen when we said he was sick? Was there more we could have done? How is any of this usable? Anger and fear threaten to fill the emptiness.

But every day we talk. Every day I post my journey. Every day we are intentional with Daniel and Natalie. Every day I try to engage the day with hope and allow God to fill the emptiness.

Being still is when the doubts begin to arise for me. Yet, God commands me to quiet my spirit and know that he is God. Uncertainty and a lack of trust often cause me to sin or not bring my troubles to Him. God is not intimidated by doubt. He points me back to his character and follows through even when we doubt. In Luke, the disciples witnessed the resurrected Jesus standing before them and struggled to believe. I am grateful that God does not leave me stuck. Instead, He shows up during my doubting.

In the verses following Luke 24:36 Jesus:

- Acknowledged and challenged their doubt.

- Declared I am indeed the resurrected Christ, not a ghost. He invited them to touch his wounds.

- Sat down and ate a meal with them. (A ghost does not eat food.)

- Gave them a refresher course on everything he taught them.

- Opened their minds to the truth of scripture and its fulfillment.

- Declared them witnesses to his suffering and resurrection and his call to repentance and forgiveness of sins.

- Gave instructions on how to share their witness with the nations.

From this, I conclude:

- Jesus is not intimidated by my doubt.

- He will prove himself to me.

- He will remind me of everything he has done for me.

- He will teach me through example, scripture, and fulfilling his promises.

- He expects me to witness what I have seen and heard.

Turning Your Page

There is only one way to deal with doubts. Trust through them. Jesus does not abandon you but asks that you keep your eyes fixed on Him.

How did God work through the disciples' doubts?

List doubts you have in grief.

Meditate on scripture and speak truth over your doubts.

Pray With Me:

When doubts surface, reveal any hidden fears or false beliefs in me. Thank you for still performing miracles in my indecision. Teach me to put faith and trust in your love.

Amen

Playlist:

"Even If" by Kutless

Lifted by Music

Those who trust in the LORD are like Mount Zion, which cannot be moved, but abides forever.
Psalm 125:1

Before I met Jesus at the age of twenty, I listened to music that celebrated my depression and encouraged my downward spiral. I liked hearing someone else repeatedly sing the cycle of my sad emotions because I thought they understood my pain. Once Jesus moved his stereo system into my house, I heard the words for the first time and felt the weight of hopelessness. I began listening to life-giving music that still acknowledged difficult things but gave me scripture and truth and humbled me. The songs, *It is Well* by Horatio Spafford, *Liberty* by Shane & Shane, and *Held* by Natalie Grant are examples of music that became my heart's cry as I grieved Jonathan. They each point out that there is so much more story to write beyond my loss.

Turning My Page

My world is dark, and I need a good anthem to lift my head and cry out to a God who hears my song. Music causes me to look beyond what I feel, see beyond the battlefield of depression, and open my soul to the possibility of finding joy again. Lord, I will find joy again!

Family and friends are sending me songs, such as David Dunn's "Today is Beautiful," as sparks of encouragement. These songs express that God is with me, knows my pain, and I do not have to walk this path of grief alone. In my shock, I can't process day-to-day life well, but my soul still leans into hope through music that points back to God.

Turning Your Page

Songs, at their core, are testimonies of our observations and experiences. Start looking for songs to meditate on. Do you feel your soul-stirring? Dance, sob, laugh. Allow the music to reveal your deepest emotions. Sing to a God who cares and connects with your songs of lament and praise.

What are some of your favorite songs that lift your spirits and encourage you through your day?

Pick out a new artist to listen to.

If you have not considered the lyrics you are listening to, write some of them down.

Pray With Me:

Father, you minister through music. Tune my ear to worship's effect on my grief. I feel lonely, tempted to despair, and isolated. Lead me to songs that lift my soul and remind me of your faithfulness.

Amen

Playlist:

"Because He Lives" by Matt Maher

Planted by the Lord

Instead of mourning, the garment of praise
instead of a faint spirit; that they may
be called oaks of righteousness, the planting
of the LORD, that he may be glorified.
Isaiah 61:3b

"Therefore, as you received Christ Jesus the Lord, so walk in him, rooted and built up in him and established in the faith, just as you were taught, abounding in thanksgiving" (Colossians 2:6-7).

The Jonathan tree, now taller and nine years older than when our community gifted it to us, has weathered many storms. It had been doubled over by wind and ice, and I held my breath, hoping it would survive some rough nights. Still, that little tree grows and thrives, encouraging me so much when I can't see my growth. God is at work strengthening me.

Turning My Page

My neighbors presented me with an oak tree in Jonathan's honor. What a unique symbol of what I long to become. Oak trees are known for growing slowly and steadily over many years, and their wood is thick and solid. They grow their roots downward and are less likely to be uprooted by storms. I have grown discouraged in the past week, overcome by the lack of sleep and my new normal without Jonathan. I feel withered!

The tree reminds me that I didn't plant myself. The Lord planted me here. He has a purpose in my sufferings, which most certainly includes bringing life out of death. I continue to allow him to water me and give me the nutrition I need through prayer, scripture, and fellowship so that I can witness his love, discipline, and plan for our lives.

May my life and my family's lives be a beautiful display of God's splendor so that many more trees can be planted and called oaks of righteousness.

Turning Your Page

You were planted in the deep and rich soil of God's love. You are an oak of righteousness when you choose to grieve with hope.

How does knowing that God planted you in your current circumstances change grief for the better?

Do you feel more secure that the Lord has planted you as an oak of righteousness for his glory?

What do you need to sustain yourself in grief?

Pray With Me:

Thank you, Lord, for planting me in these circumstances. Help me to be a light in the darkness.

Amen

Playlist:

"He Will" by Ellie Holcomb

Putting on a Cloak of Praise in Grief

*You have turned for me my mourning into dancing; you
have loosed my sackcloth and clothed me with gladness,
that my glory may sing your praise and not be silent.
O LORD my God, I will give thanks to you forever!
Psalm 30:11-12*

M y family can tell when I have worn a cloak of praise by the
fruits of my daily attitude. It is a marked intentionality. I
put on a mantle of praise by getting up and having my quiet time,
stepping outside into nature, and singing. Grief is no match for j
oy.

Turning My Page

I encourage you to read Psalm 30. David knew what
sorrow was. Sackcloth was a rough, uncomfortable
material that mourners wore to signify their deep
distress. He had a lot of loss, some caused by others
and some by his hand. He did much mourning, but
he also was disciplined about praising God. Praise,
whether wailing or dancing.

We have a concrete image of a garment of sorrow,
but I wonder what a garment of joy looks like. I
keep picturing Joseph's coat of many colors. Jacob,

Joseph's father, put the coat on his son as a symbol of his great pleasure. It was a celebration of all Joseph was to him!

My garment of joy would be in emerald greens and deep red wine colors (my wedding colors) and have golden words embroidered into the fabric, Words like creative, love, joy, passion, laughter, peace, faith, and compassion. These things in my life cause me to want to dance.

I remember hearing a story from a friend about a scientist boss who wore a white lab coat with creative ideas written all over it. He wore it when he wanted to create something new and inspire his team. Yesterday, I saw a man in a t-shirt celebrating an old car show gathering in Eastern Kentucky. I wish I had taken a picture of it because it was filled with his enjoyment of cars.

When we wear a garment of joy, we want to praise! It is contagious. I had several friends yesterday snap me out of my downward spiral and remind me of the creative possibilities when I put on my garment of joy. Thank you, I will be dancing today!

Turning Your Page

Putting on a garment of praise may be hard for you today. But you do not dress because you feel like it, dress in joy, peace, patience, and kindness because life is still filled with creative possibility.

What do you think a garment of joy would look like for you? What colors would be in it? Would there be words or images? How can you put on a garment of praise?

Come up with three or four words to describe the joy you want as you grieve.

Maybe you need to ask God to give you the desire to experience joy.

Pray With Me:

Father, thank you for such a vivid image of joy. Teach me to put on this spirit as I grieve so that others can see the impossible made possible.

Amen

Playlist:

"Garments" by Cory Asbury

The Changing Cells of Faith

And he said to them, "Follow me,
and I will make you fishers of men."
Matthew 4:19

I speak to medical staff, pastors, lay leaders, students, teachers, and community warriors about mental health from the parent and layperson perspective. Vulnerability keeps the wound of Jonathan's death fresh because people are hungry to know what to do and how they can help. Though I get weary of the harsh reality of despair, I never tire of offering hope. God's closeness to our despair energizes me. I see the evidence in scripture and my personal experience. He hears my cry. He knows my heart aches for peace and healing, and he opens my eyes to the needs of others.

Turning My Page

Our physical bodies regenerate cell by cell every two years. What if the same is true of our spiritual health? Jesus trained the disciples for three years, and then they were ready to preach to the nations. They went from undisciplined, quarreling, and self-centered to a team, a powerhouse of faith.

I desire a change in the pattern of suicide. Improvement in the current treatment system for depression is necessary, and the church should be involved. Within three years, Jesus could fully train and prepare believers to curb the tide of suicide. We need God to heal our hearts. I am learning so much by walking with Jesus daily and allowing his ways to become mine.

Jesus did not pick the religious leaders of the time for his disciples because they were entrenched in their ways of thinking. They would not follow. The son of God chose men and women hungry for God's presence, even though they didn't fully understand his message.

Turning Your Page

There are God-ordained possibilities in great suffering. By studying examples of those who suffered and yet stood firm in faith— both in scripture and current testimonies—you can find the strength to turn the page on your loved one's suicide. Two years from now, as you grieve with hope, you will not be the person you were in the depth of fresh sorrow.

What qualities do you observe in how others grieve around you? List the similarities and differences.

How is your grief similar to the prophet Ezra in Ezra 9, King David in Psalm 31, and Jesus in John 11?

By sharing your story of hope, how can you encourage others? A Grief Share or survivor's support group in your area can give you a community of people in various grief stages.

Pray With Me:

I am not the same as I was at the start of grieving. Lord, thank you that I can share hope while still experiencing pain.

Amen

Playlist:

"Way Maker" by Mandisa

Grief, A Patchwork of Remembering Rightly

Therefore, if anyone is in Christ, he is a new creation.
The old has passed away; behold, the new has come.
All this is from God, who through Christ reconciled us
to himself and gave us the ministry of reconciliation.
2 Corinthians 5:17-18

My story is a patchwork quilt of experiences. Since those early days of grief, new squares have been added. Photography, something I never explored before my son's death, is now a regular part of the way that I connect to God and encourage others. New friendships have developed out of my grief. I've been a part of others choosing to embrace hope when tempted to despair. I have written hundreds of poems and devotions, and I feel God's closeness more deeply. God is creating something new through writing devotions, teaching me to speak boldly about depression and suicide, and in his love for the oppressed. Jonathan's death is a square in my quilt; its colors are vivid, but his suicide doesn't tell the whole story. My hopes and dreams for Jonathan are gone. My hope in God's salvation story is far from over.

Turning My Page

Memories are a patchwork quilt. They contain many layers of experiences sewn together to form something new. My grandmother made several quilts and gave them to my family. Each swatch of fabric was from clothes she wore. They held memories of her, but they were put together to create a new memory of her for me. The same thing is happening to my family and me.

Daniel will be wearing Jonathan's LSU shirt tomorrow. He is so excited, but seeing him as big enough to wear his brother's clothes is hard. God reconciles my memories of Jonathan by sewing our experiences together to make something new for Brian, Daniel, Natalie, and me. I can either hold to the fabric as a painful reminder of what I've lost or allow God to put together a patchwork of reconciliation. Through my sorrow, I hold each quilt piece loosely and choose to see what God patches together for others.

Turning Your Page

You may feel like your life is in pieces. Scraps of memories surround you, and you're unsure what to do with these remnants. Allow God to create a new framework for your sorrow. His masterpiece considers your sorrow and includes it as a square, not a whole quilt. Lay out what you hold most dear about your loved one and ask God to create something new.

What special memories of your loved one would you like to transform into new memories for the present? Can pictures be pulled out to display?

Create a garden or picture display in their honor.

How are you doing with finalizing your loved one's affairs? Settle the things that must be done immediately, but there is no rush in packing their belongings. Do this as you can.

Pray With Me:

Creator, you are piecing together a masterpiece from what is, and my sorrow is a part of your design. Help me remember my loved ones for the beautiful squares they are. I wait expectantly for the glorious unveiling of the whole quilt.

Amen

Playlist:

"My Story Your Glory" by Matthew West

Showing Mercy in Grief

Count it all joy, my brothers, when you meet
trials of various kinds, because you know that
the testing of your faith develops perseverance.
And let steadfastness have its full effect, that you
may be perfect and complete, lacking in nothing.
James 1:2-3

I'll be honest with you: I'm not at the place yet where I "count it all joy," as James says, but grief has given me lots of opportunities to persevere. Sometimes, people said incredibly hurtful or insensitive things, and others simply didn't know I was grieving and were reacting out of their own wounds. It was easy to growl at people, and sometimes even felt good to let someone have it. But only for a moment. Rather than an intentional God-directed response, reactiveness does more harm than good. The constant rub of trials causes me to look to scripture for examples of steadfastness, and I am deeply encouraged by the response of the early church. They show me it is possible to show mercy when others do not, not because it comes naturally, but because Jesus laid down his life for me when I didn't deserve mercy.

Turning My Page

My family missed our connection from Dallas to Houston due to no fault of our own and potentially faced a six-hour wait until we could board another plane. We were exhausted and emotional. We just wanted to go home. We went to Houston to see friends and get away from the heartache for a bit, but getting stuck only revealed our raw emotions. No one at the airline was especially kind or made any effort to get us home any sooner.

With my new heartbreak, anger flared, and I was tempted to return the unkindness. I began grumbling under my breath and fed my frustration, but the Holy Spirit stepped in and gently nudged, are you seeing them as I see them?

I knew I didn't see them as the Holy Spirit did, and I certainly wasn't counting this trial as joyful. The Lord brought to mind the early church's response to their trial of persecution described in James. I realized the lack of kindness, justice, and mercy I was experiencing in the airport was not an excuse to be hurtful back. I had an opportunity to show the gate agents the love of Jesus through kindness, justice, and mercy by patiently waiting, not speaking ill, and being pleasant to my family.

I was inconvenienced, not threatened. I stood at the counter, recognized the humanity in the surly woman in front of me, smiled, and prayed for God to move me with compassion for her. Grief frayed my emotions, but I can still show mercy when at other people's mercy.

Turning Your Page

Unkindness is not a character flaw. We all have sins we are naturally drawn to, but training ourselves to engage our world differently is possible. Grief reveals those inconsistencies and is a fantastic opportunity to respond well. What are your current temptations? It can be helpful to list them so that you slowly become more aware of any actions inconsistent with your character.

What are your current reactions to difficult people and situations?

What small steps can you take to curb wrong thinking about others or actions you catch yourself taking when stressed?

You will react wrongly at times. Apologize when you can, and extend grace to yourself as you develop your character.

Pray With Me:

Lord, a lot of things have not gone as I expected. I feel frustrated. Help me to dwell on what is good.

Amen

Playlist:

"The Struggle" by Tenth Avenue North

God Keeps Watch

*Then he who saw cried out: "Upon a watchtower
I stand, O Lord, continually by day, and
at my post I am stationed whole nights.
Isaiah 21:8*

D ifficulty sleeping and nightmares often follow a tragic loss. I want to say this many years into my journey that I have had no disrupted nights, but I do. I am more equipped to speak the truth over nightmares and ask questions. Have I started neglecting good sleep hygiene? Am I dwelling on regret? Is there someone I need to forgive? Do I need to remember my son in a new way? How can I praise God when I don't sleep? These questions remind me that my lack of sleep does not have the final say.

Turning My Page

No sleep last night. Not a wink. I lay there in the stillness. I don't remember thinking anything as I held my eyes closed. Numbness is most certainly not the same thing as rest. I haven't felt well for the past two days, and I don't know if that led to my poor night of sleep.

I didn't even try to reach out to God. I'm not sure I could, and that's okay. He knows sometimes we can't reach out. Jesus was God's hand, reaching out for me before I could grasp that love. Even when I cannot reach out to him, I feel secure that he loves me.

I've looked at my lifetime of battling insomnia as a curse. What if it is a blessing? As the crickets chirp outside my window, I can offer you hope on a night when you, too, may lay awake. You may have felt the weight of your circumstances closing in on you. You may feel as if you have no hope.

Let me be your night watchman! Let me hold the light of truth up to your circumstances. There is absolutely nothing God cannot handle! Nothing can separate you from his love!

Turning Your Page

Be careful with caffeinated drinks and heavy foods. Good sleep hygiene strengthens you for the long road of grief. Form good habits that are not optional while you grieve.

How are you sleeping? Do you look at the restless nights as an opportunity to pray?

Many throughout scripture had nights of no sleep, including Jesus. Meditate on their response to sleepless nights.

Pray With Me:

Lord, my body needs sleep. May nothing hinder refreshing my body, but may I continue to glorify you if it does.

Amen

Playlist:

"Watch Over Me" by Jason Upton

Throwing Out the Spirit of Fear

*When I am afraid, I put my trust in you. In God,
whose word I praise, in God I trust; I shall not be
afraid. What can flesh do to me? For you have
delivered my soul from death, yes, my feet from failing.
That I may walk before God in the light of life.*
Psalm 56:3-4, 13

Since Jonathan's death, I have had multiple near-death experiences, the worst being multiple clots filling my lungs. Fearing death and loss is a constant temptation. The horrid reality is suicide has swallowed up marriages, siblings, fathers and mothers, friends, and so many more. I must remain vigilant. There is a battle beyond what my eyes can see, and I find security in knowing God is fighting for me. I love agreeing with his plan and watching him move what once seemed impossible. I am learning to sharpen the weapons of spiritual warfare: prayer, scripture, truth, salvation, and the gospel of peace (Ephesians 6:10-18) because my fight isn't against flesh and blood. My battle is against the spiritual realm that seeks to crush us. I continue to fight the spirit of despair, but I am now stronger and quicker to use the sword of the Spirit (scripture) against this persistent enemy.

Turning My Page

Whatever it takes to remove the spirit of fear in my house, Lord, I am willing to do. Both children and I are currently plagued by nightmares. Daniel and I were up about the same time, crying out from our dreams last night. Daniel has also started struggling with tantrums and is getting in trouble at school. We have an enemy that seeks to destroy us from an early age. I have struggled with severe nightmares since childhood that led to fear taking root. I do not want this for my children.

Fear is the opposite of trust, so I asked the Lord this morning to reveal what is happening in our home. He gave me a few very clear directions. One, there is a spirit of depression and fear in our home, which must be cleared out for us to rest well.

Secondly, I needed to remove an item. Daniel and Jonathan shared a room, and Daniel now wraps up in Jonathan's blanket instead of his own. I realize we need to clean the room, repaint it, and make it Daniel's room. Ephesians 6 says my battle is not against flesh and blood. The enemy can attack my family clearly and subtly through the spirit we allow into our home.

I don't know if removing Jonathan's things from the room will help Daniel's nightmares stop, but I know that Jonathan's blanket was brought to mind when I asked the Lord. If having the blanket in the room keeps Daniel trapped in the nightmare of his brother's death, I am more than happy to remove it. I will trust God and teach my children to do the same when I am afraid. Thank you, Lord, for equipping us as parents and making the unseen visible.

(UPDATE) After removing the blanket, Daniel's nightmares ceased. He didn't miss or ever ask about the blanket.

Turning Your Page

Do nightmares plague you? Scripture talks about the oppression of the spirit of fear. You are not helpless to fight this spirit. Trust God more and more with your grief. You will find rest in and through him no matter the battle.

Pray through the rooms of your home, asking God if anything contributes to the spirit of despair. It may take a while for the spirit to leave, or it may occur immediately. Do not grow weary. You have all of heaven fighting with you.

Meditate on Romans 8:2 Timothy 1:7, and Psalm 91. Write your thoughts here.

Pray With Me:

Lord, help me to throw off the blanket of fear that threatens to smother your will in my life. Help me to listen to your wise counsel when I open the door to the spirit of despair.

Amen

Playlist:

"My Deliverer" by Chris Tomlin

Surprised by Joy in the Mourning

*And you became imitators of us and of the Lord, for
you received the word in much affliction with the joy
of the Holy Spirit, so that you became an example
to all the believers in Macedonia and in Acacia.*
1 Thessalonians 1:6-7

The Holy Spirit is my best friend and constant teacher. I lean into him as I write and struggle, and his voice becomes more evident daily. There is no going through grief without my constant counselor. He carries me when I feel I can't take one step more and offers joy when all I experience should crush my soul.

Turning My Page

Yesterday, I woke up without the heaviness of Jonathan's death weighing down my heart, and this morning, again, I had the same feeling. I am surprised. All day yesterday, I kept expecting to feel the pressure return. Instead, I remembered wonderful moments with Jonathan, laughed at my children's antics, and experienced a deep joy that didn't make sense. Joy was a gift from the Comforter.

Turning Your Page

I pray that joy begins to replace the constant mantra of sorrow in your suffering. It truly is a gift that may surprise you one morning, not because you stop missing your loved one but because you see Christ in the new day.

How do you define joy?

Describe a good moment this week where you laughed or connected with someone.

If you are not feeling moments of joy yet, keep walking through each day, embrace new opportunities, and wait expectantly for joy to come.

Pray With Me:

Father, it is hard to believe I can breathe, let alone feel joy, yet here you are, gifting me with the impossible. I praise you, my portion, and my rescuer!

Amen

Playlist:

"Trading My Sorrows" by Darrell Evans

Imitation: The Best Form of Flattering God

Therefore be imitators of God, as beloved children.
And walk in love, as Christ loved us and gave Himself
up for us, a fragrant offering and sacrifice to God.
Ephesians 5:1-2

I am so grateful I have young children who witness to me an in-color life. Faith, love, and hope are worth imitating. My son and daughter poke holes in my serious attitude, teach me to play, and breathe deeply the refreshing love of God. They ask questions about grief, which I am often afraid to ask. When I engage my world through grief, I feel heaven lean in, breathe deeply, and love me.

Turning My Page

My children created a salon yesterday, and though they made me a bit nervous with the scissors, they assured me they would not cut each other's hair. Much of what they learn is by imitation, and imitation is how I am learning to be like Christ as I grieve.

In my grief, I don't always reflect on Ephesians 5: 1-2. Instead, I more accurately look like Ephesians 4:31-32—bitter, dwelling on hurts, wanting revenge on those who hurt my son, and angry. Thank God for the "therefore" between these two chapters. Therefore (as a result of) implies I can change. I can acknowledge my sin, put on the attitude of Christ, and imitate his kindness, tender-heartedness, and forgiveness. I take this step of obedience, even when I'm not fully on board with the outcome.

When I remember the tenderness, Christ showed me when I didn't deserve forgiveness, praying blessings for my enemies and looking beyond my circumstances for the goodness of God became my desire. Through imitation, I learn and grow and show the grace I have been given.

Just as I smiled, watching my children mimic the salon, my Father in Heaven delights in imitation. One day, I will no longer be imitating. I will walk in love, and others will see God because I am imitating his son.

Turning Your Page

There is no greater time to imitate Christ than when we wish the cup of grief to pass from us. Daily we must declare not my will, which leads to death, but God's will, the path to resurrection.

What characteristics of Christ do you want to work most on in imitating Christ in your grief?

How can friends and family help you as you work towards imitating Christ?

Who is holding you accountable?

Pray With Me:

Father, may I become a sweet fragrance to others because I have spent time snuggling close to and learning from you daily.

Amen

Playlist:

"To Be Like You" by Hillsong

Creation Gives Comfort in Grief

But ask the beasts, and they will teach you; the birds of the heavens, and they will tell you; or the bushes of the earth, and they will teach you; and the fish of the sea will declare to you. Who among all these does not know that the hand of the LORD has done this? In his hand is the life of every living thing and the breath of all mankind.
Job 12:7-10

God has comforted me through my husband, children, friends, sermons, and scripture. But the Creator knows nature is one place where I have my ear to the ground listening to his voice. It is a quiet place for me. Nature, like a tangible love note from God, reminds me that he sees me; my grief is not distant from him. Creation testifies to God's goodness everywhere I look, and I am so grateful he chooses to invite me into his presence through nature's sanctuary.

Turning My Page

I took a rose to Jonathan's grave this morning. Walking towards the grave, I spotted a doe with her fawn grazing several rows beyond. I froze and watched them. The grounds crew was working just across the road and must have seen what was happening because they stopped their motors.

Rather than running away, the doe looked right at me and walked steadily toward me. I sobbed as I saw the fawn following her mother and remembered the love Jonathan and I shared.

Even when I resumed walking towards the grave, they walked up just above the head of the grave. They never invaded my space but stood only yards away, paying their respects to my son and giving me a beautiful love note from my Heavenly Father.

Peace washed over me.

Turning Your Page

From the crocus who emerges in the cold death of winter, to the ocean teeming with life, nature testifies to God's presence, provision, and power over life and death. In grief, it can be easy to stop noticing the things that testify to God's power over your circumstances. Look out your window, take a walk, and ask God to show his goodness and comfort to you through what you witness in nature. God will let you know that he is present with you. Even if it is hard to see now, look back at your childhood. Were there ways you were in awe of nature? Record a moment you were aware of his presence in nature.

Meditate on Luke 12:22-31 and record your thoughts here.

What are ways God comforts you in grief through nature?

List small and big ways God testifies to his power over life and death in nature.

Pray With Me:

Creator, this beautiful earth testifies that you provide for me. Open my eyes to your goodness in nature. Help me to remember that you value me and will bring life out of my loss.

Amen

Playlist:

"Praise the Lord (Psalm 150)" by Shane & Shane

Filling What's Missing With Love

Oh, the depth of the riches and wisdom and knowledge of God! How unsearchable are His judgments, and how inscrutable his ways! For who has known the mind of the Lord, or who has been his counselor?
Romans 11:33-34

Jonathan is always missing in my pictures, but I can tell you what isn't—love, faith, and hope. Loving and being loved fills my heart with joy. Faith creates an algorithm for grief, and hope keeps me waiting expectantly to see God's glory show up in my life. He never disappoints.

Turning My Page

Today was our church picnic, and I looked at the beautiful picture of friends and family as if a person had been cut out. I loved being there, but my heart ached deeply to hear Jonathan's voice, to have him beat me at kickball, and to laugh at my rusty attempt at rollerblading.

Life is a beautiful picture of people and circumstances. We fit together like a puzzle, and the picture seems incomplete when someone is suddenly gone. But even as I say that, I realize it isn't the "Jonathan piece" I'm missing. He is a part of my life picture. What is missing is the outcome I thought my son should have. The picture of his life turned out differently than I expected.

God's ways are not mine. His ideas on what is just, fair, good, and evil in my life are much different. I don't understand how Jonathan's death works to glorify God. I am like a child who is told to take something good for me and turn up my nose because I know it tastes awful.

My five-year-old daughter had to take a particularly nasty-tasting antibiotic. I told her the medicine would fight the infection in her foot, but it didn't matter. She could not get past the taste and tried to refuse the treatment. My picture and hers were much different on the medication. She thought it was bad, and I knew it was good for her.

What if my circumstances turn the tide of suicide? I keep offering hope to you through these pages. I keep training to provide hope on a larger scale. But I don't know what God has in store, and I realize my puzzle is incomplete. I must allow Him to develop the picture of who I am and how my circumstances fit together.

Turning Your Page

Death was not a part of God's original plan for creation, but mankind introduced it through disobedience. There is no way to resurrection except through death. The hardness of grief remains for you, but God is faithful as you grieve.

How does grief fit into God's big picture of humanity? Read Romans 3:23, 6:23, and Romans 8:11.

What are ways you see God using your grief for your good?

Create a collage. Include pictures of your loved one and write out beside them ways your life changed for the better because he/she lived. Add verses that speak to how Jesus is helping you walk through grief because of his life, death, and resurrection.

Pray With Me:

Father, this sorrow hurts more than I can bear, but because I know you bore the cross for me, I will stand under the weight of all I feel, knowing you understand my suffering.

Amen

Playlist:

"Man of Sorrows" by Ellie Holcomb

Anticipating God's Goodness

*"I believe that I shall look upon the goodness
of the LORD in the land of the living!
Wait for the LORD; be strong, and let your
heart take courage; wait for the LORD!"
Psalm 27:13-14*

A key ingredient to grieving well is knowing God is good and anticipating his good gifts in grief. The most challenging days I experienced were the ones I closed myself off to the possibility of realizing hope. When I opened my heart, no matter how deep the ache, I was surprised and delighted by joy, insights from friends, laughter, and God's love.

Turning My Page

Since the first day I turned the page on my son's suicide and kept writing my story, each day has brought new circumstances. Some are good, and some seem bad, but I commit daily to engage life rather than withdrawing from feeling.

I'm not sure what today has in store, but as I dropped the kids off at school and headed toward the café to write, I felt the tingle of anticipation and excitement.

"Excitement for what, Lord?" I asked. "What do you have in store for me today?" Surprised by the feeling, I praised him, even though he's not revealed his plan for my day.

The emotion feels like anticipating a surprise on my birthday. I know God always gives the best gifts. I don't know the contents of each package or the arrival time, but I know God's promise. Maybe it is the gift of himself. Oh, the pleasure—God, my heavenly daddy, sits across from me, and I fellowship with him. Just the thought gives me chills.

My anticipation of God's presence is grounded in taking every thought captive and making it obedient to Christ. I started this morning with a dark cloud hovering over me as I surveyed all I needed to accomplish today. Instead of letting the storm break, I dispersed it with the truth. I looked at my husband and children and was filled with love for them. I chose to laugh and be patient with my tired and cranky son. I anticipate God's goodness today because he is good.

Turning Your Page

With the shock of loss comes cynicism. You have experienced a very negative trauma, and dark thoughts come out of shock when feelings begin to reengage. Don't let darkness linger. Speak truth over your thought patterns quickly and consistently.

Exercise truth like a muscle, and God strengthens your mind to recognize the good things he has in store for you.

Do you anticipate God's good gifts?

Do you look for the worst or best to happen?

Begin recording the good things happening in your life. Don't forget to include the minor details.

Pray With Me:

Lord, you are good. You are good. You are good! In these bad circumstances of grief help me to anticipate your goodness and embrace joy when it comes.

Amen

Playlist:

"Joy Comes in the Morning" by Tauren Wells

Who is Your Exit Buddy?

For if they fall, one will lift up his fellow.
But woe to him who is alone when he
falls and has not another to lift him up!
Ecclesiastes 4:10

W hen I learned my son was dead, my home quickly filled with people who cried with me, held my family, and let me grieve. They encouraged me to move through the valley of the shadow of death but not take up residence there. It wasn't easy to accept help, but even in those early days, I recognized the danger of isolating myself. I needed people. Friends weeded my garden, some took me out to change my environment, and others challenged my wrong thinking. They showed me Christ in tangible ways. Years later, it still amazes me when a friend sends me a text at the exact moment my thoughts spiral and I am weary. I do not regret allowing friends to walk with me during gr ief.

Turning My Page

Who is your exit buddy? In the animated movie *Finding Nemo* (Unkrich, 2003), Dory is Marlin's exit buddy. Crush, the turtle, prepares Marlin to exit the East Australian Current, and Marlin freaks out. Dory remained by his side for almost the entire search for his son Nemo and encouraged Marlin to "just keep swimming" when he felt like giving up. Just as the story provided Marlin with an exit buddy,

Christ provides companionship for me. Friends and strangers lift me up when my burden grows heavy.

I am grateful for my exit buddies. Men and women ride the current of grief with me and teach me to live more deeply. They see the exit, even if I can't. One friend invited me to join a painting class with her. I don't paint. But it gave me a quiet space to engage the world in a new way and time to connect with other creatives. Another gave my husband and me the freedom to speak openly about our son Jonathan. She always asked, "What's one thing you miss about Jonathan? What's a favorite memory?" Expecting good things is not a part of my DNA, and grief can easily bring out the Marlin worrier in me, but I keep learning from my friends. They love me well and carry me to the cross to witness the reaction of Jesus to suffering.

Jesus was God in the flesh, yet he cultivated exit buddies. His disciples were imperfect men and women but remained Christ's constant companions until the garden arrest. Without my friends, I could not survive these first days or the many days to come. They pull me into adventures and out of the pit of despair. I live more fully because they aren't afraid to enter my painful circumstances.

Turning Your Page

If you don't have an exit buddy, I encourage you to find one. Who in your life drives you crazy with a never-give-up attitude? A safe bet is when they are around, you find yourself doing things you thought impossible. You need friends. Imperfect, sometimes in-your-face friends who let you know you've gotten too focused on grief and lost sight of the fact there is a big ocean of possibilities.

How has your exit buddy helped you see the possibilities in life or escape depression?

In what specific ways can you be an exit buddy to someone else?

Do you have a friend who helps you move through grief? Write a thank-you note and express how they have encouraged you.

Pray With Me:

Father, you surround me with witnesses who challenge me to grow and mature in faith. I praise you. I do not go through this vast ocean of grief alone because you gifted me, friends, to journey with me. Thank you.

Amen

Playlist:

"Meet Me There" by Lydia Laird

From Ashes to Beauty

*To grant to those who mourn in Zion— to
give them a beautiful headdress instead of ashes,
the oil of gladness instead of mourning, the
garment of praise instead of a faint spirit; that
they may be called oaks of righteousness, the
planting of the LORD, that he may be glorified.
Isaiah 61:3b*

Can God do anything with the ashes of your loss? Yes. You may not see the beauty after sixty days of grieving, but if you place your heart and expectations in God's goodness, you will not be disappointed.

Years into a life without my son, God proves himself trustworthy. I laugh, develop new good memories, and learn to view my son's death as only a speck in a more extraordinary story. In this life, strife and heartache attempt to crush our spirit, but take heart because God has overcome the world (John 16:33). Continue to write your story.

Turning My Page

Yesterday was a lots-of-tears day. Grief will be a lifetime experience because I will never stop missing my son. Many of us have lost loved ones; death comes in many forms. So how do we keep from being sucked into despair as we grieve?

Isaiah 61:3 has been a life verse for eighteen years and answers the question. Receive God-given comfort, beauty, joy, and praise. When I feel shaken, I remember God gives me good gifts in my suffering. Isaiah, a prophet, not only gave Israel hope but hinted at the Messiah to come. I don't get sucked into despair because God replaces my ashes with beauty, turning my mourning into gladness and despair into praise through his son, Jesus Christ.

Turning Your Page

Nothing is impossible for God. Do you struggle to believe this statement? Scripture declares God's capabilities from beginning to end. Here are examples: Genesis 18:14, Numbers 23:19, Isaiah 40:2, Zechariah 9:12, Romans 5:5, Titus 1:2, Hebrews 3:6, Hebrews 6:17-19, Revelation 7:8-10.

Look back through your journaling. Take a highlighter and mark any record of God doing great things through your grief in the last sixty days.

What awful things has God already made beautiful in your grief?

Practice praising God. You can do this by singing to worship music or saying or praying a verse out loud. Develop a thankful list.

Pray With Me:

I praise you, Lord. I believe you will bring life out of my loved one's death. You are not through with me yet. I praise you. Your love and comfort will encourage and equip me in my darkest hours. I praise you.

Amen

Playlist:

"Even This Will Be Made Beautiful" by Jason Gray

Bonus: Writing a Psalm of Sustenance in Grief

In one of my devotions, I mentioned that psalms were a balm. They taught me to lament well. I often wrote my own psalms in response to what scripture revealed through my lament.

Fill My Grief
by Karisa Moore

I held out my hands for my daily bread,
Not knowing what provision would come,
But knowing You would send sustenance.

I held my heart out like a cup,
Not knowing how my emptiness would be filled,
But knowing You would fill it to overflowing.

I opened my mind to Your will,
Not knowing where You would lead my thoughts,
But knowing that Your thoughts expand my universe.

I opened my mouth for Your words,
Not knowing which ones You would feed me,
But knowing that they would not go out and come
back void.

Turning Your Page

I encourage you to pour out your heart as you grieve. The psalmist included the following:

Observations of nature

Reminders of what the psalmist knew of God

Acknowledged their plight

Reminders to rejoice in who God is

If you choose to write a Psalm about your grief, here are questions to prompt your thoughts.

What do you already know about God?

What is God teaching you about yourself or others as you grieve?

How is God sustaining you?

Practice thankfulness.

Pray With Me:

Lord, I pray over our journey as we walk through grief. Knowing you walk with me and that there is someone else aware of my sorrow.

Amen

Scriptures For Meditation

The LORD is near to the brokenhearted and saves the crushed in spirit. Psalm 34:18

For his anger is but for a moment, and his favor is for a lifetime. Weeping may tarry for the night, but joy comes with the morning. Psalm 30:5

But we have this treasure in jars of clay, to show that the surpassing power belongs to God and not to us. We are afflicted in every way, but not crushed; perplexed, but not driven to despair; persecuted, but not forsaken; struck down, but not destroyed; always carrying in the body the death of Jesus, so that the life of Jesus may also be manifested in our bodies. 2 Corinthians 4:7-10

For my father and my mother have forsaken me, but the LORD will take me in. Psalm 27:10

But now thus says the LORD, he who created you, O Jacob, he who formed you, O Israel: "Fear not, for I have redeemed you; I have called you by name, you are mine. When you pass through the waters, I will be with you; and through the rivers, they shall not overwhelm you; when you walk through fire you shall not be burned, and the flame shall not consume you. Isaiah 43:1-2

Behold, I am doing a new thing; now it springs forth, do you not perceive it? I will make a way in the wilderness and rivers in the desert. Isaiah 43:19

I will restore to you the years that the swarming locust has eaten, the hopper, the destroyer, and the cutter, my great army, which I sent among you. You shall eat in plenty and be satisfied, and praise the name of the LORD your God, who has dealt wondrously with you. And my people shall never again be put to shame. You shall know that I am in the midst of Israel, and that I am the LORD your God and there is none else. And my people shall never again be put to shame. Joel 2:25-27

So to keep me from becoming conceited because of the surpassing greatness of the revelations, a thorn was given me in the flesh, a messenger of Satan to harass me, to keep me from becoming conceited. Three times I pleaded with the Lord about this, that it should leave me. But he said to me, 'My grace is sufficient for you, for my power is made perfect in weakness.' Therefore I will boast all the more gladly of my weaknesses, so that the power of Christ may rest upon me. 2 Corinthians 12:7-9

For we were so utterly burdened beyond our strength that we despaired of life itself. Indeed, we felt that we had received the sentence of death. But that was to make us rely not on ourselves but on God who raises the dead. 2 Corinthians 1:8-9

I believe that I shall look upon the goodness of the LORD in the land of the living! Wait for the LORD; be strong, and let your heart take courage; wait for the LORD! Psalm 27:13-14

Why are you cast down, O my soul, and why are you in turmoil within me? Hope in God; for I shall again praise him, my salvation and my God. Psalm 43:5

So we do not lose heart. Though our outer self is wasting away, our inner self is being renewed day by day. For this light momentary affliction is preparing for us an eternal weight of glory beyond all comparison, as we look not to the things that are seen but to the things that are unseen. For the things that are seen are transient, but the things that are unseen are eternal. 2 Corinthians 4:16-18

For the Lord will not cast off forever, but, though he cause grief, he will have compassion according to the abundance of his steadfast love;

for he does not afflict from his heart or grieve the children of men. Lamentations 3:31-33

My flesh and my heart may fail, but God is the strength of my heart and my portion forever. Psalm 73:26

Blessed are those who mourn, for they shall be comforted. Matthew 5:4

'In my Father's house are many rooms. If it were not so, would I have told you that I go to prepare a place for you? And if I go and prepare a place for you, I will come again and will take you to myself, that where I am you may be also. And you know the way to where I am going.' Thomas said to him, 'Lord, we do not know where you are going. How can we know the way?' Jesus said to him, 'I am the way, and the truth, and the life. No one comes to the Father except through me.' John 1 4:2-6

The righteous man perishes, and no one lays it to heart; devout men are taken away, while no one understands. For the righteous man is taken away from calamity; he enters into peace; they rest in their beds who walk in their uprightness. Isaiah 57:1-2

Yes, we are of good courage, and we would rather be away from the body and at home with the Lord. 2 Corinthians 5:8

Fear not, for I am with you; be not dismayed, for I am your God; I will strengthen you, I will help you, I will uphold you with my righteous right hand. Isaiah 41:10

He gives power to the faint, and to him who has no might he increases strength. Isaiah 40:20

By day the LORD commands his steadfast love, and at night his song is with me, a prayer to the God of my life. Psalm 42:8

Let your steadfast love comfort me according to your promise to your servant. Psalm 119:76

Let me hear in the morning of your steadfast love, for in you I trust. Make me know the way I should go, for to you I lift up my soul. Psalm 143:8

I believe that I shall look upon the goodness of the LORD in the land of the living! Wait for the LORD; be strong, and let your heart take courage; wait for the LORD! Psalm 27:13-14

Have I not commanded you? Be strong and courageous. Do not be frightened, and do not be dismayed, for the LORD your God is with you wherever you go. Joshua 1:8

So we do not lose heart. Though our outer self is wasting away, our inner self is being renewed day by day. For this light momentary affliction is preparing for us an eternal weight of glory beyond all comparison, as we look not to the things that are seen but to the things that are unseen. For the things that are seen are transient, but the things that are unseen are eternal. For we know that if the tent that is our earthly home is destroyed, we have a building from God, a house not made with hands, eternal in the heavens. 2 Corinthians 4:16-5:1

Notes of Encouragement from Other Grievers

"For my thoughts are not your thoughts, neither are your ways my ways, declares the LORD. For as the heavens are higher than the earth, so are my ways higher than your ways and my thoughts than your thoughts" Isaiah 55:8-9. "I would always turn to Isaiah 55: 8-9 when questioning Why."

—Karen

"And we know that for those who love God all things work together for good, for those who are called according to his purpose" (Romans 8:28). "It reminds me that God can turn any present devastation into beauty later, and that He always is working for our good, even as we can't see it."

—Whitney

"Psalm 23 says, "When I walk THROUGH the valley of the shadow of death, You are with me." The shadow can be of our death or someone else's, but God doesn't leave us in the valley of the shadow—it is somewhere we walk through together. Someday, we'll come out on the other side together. Either here or in glory. What came as a shock to me didn't surprise God. He knew the days allotted for my sweet daddy before even a single one passed. When we can't see God's plan, we trust His heart. God is good. All the time. No matter what. No. Matter. What.

—Cindee

Resourses To Help You Grieve with Hope

American Association of Christian Counselors—For Christian counseling near you, visit the directory at AACC.net
https://connect.aacc.net/?search_type=distance

Christmas Peace for Busy Moms by Sarah Geringer
https://www.sarahgeringer.com/my-books/christmas-peace-for-busy-moms/

Messy Hope: Help Your Child Overcome Anxiety, Depression, or Suicidal Ideation—Lori Wildenberg, https://loriwildenberg.com/books/messy-hope/

40 Scriptures to Combat Worry, Fear and Anxiety (free resource) by Dr. Michelle Bengtson,
https://drmichellebengtson.com/scriptures-combat-worry-fear-anxiety/

7-Day YouVersion Bible Reading Plan for Breaking Anxiety's Grip br Dr. Michelle Bengtson, How to Help a Depressed Loved One
https://drmichellebengtson.com/thank-you-for-signing-up-ebook1/

10 Things You Can Do to Counter Depression Dr. Natalie Flake Ford

https://tearstojoy.org/wp-content/uploads/2021/08/10-Things-You-Can-Do-to-Counter-Depression.pdf

Flourish-Meant Podcast Tina Yeager
https://tinayeager.com

Subdue Stress and Anxiety Course-15 Experts
https://divineencouragement.onlinecoursehost.com/courses

Local Community Resources & Crisis Hotlines
https://www.211.org/

https://www.samhsa.gov/find-help/national-helpline
1-800-662-HELP (4357)

Contact Karisa Moore at karisa@turningthepageonsuicide.org
or Snail Mail: Karisa Moore, PO Box 1288, Union, KY 41091

More Resources and Online Community

karisa@turningthepageonsuicide.org

Snail Mail: Karisa Moore, PO Box 1288, Union, KY 41091

Click or Scan QR Code for more resources from Karisa.

Link to Music

Turn the Page YouTube Play List

Scan or click the QR code to go to Turn the Page: Playlist

Bibliography

Unkrich, Lee, and Andrew Stanton. 2003. Finding Nemo. United States: Buena Vista Pictures.

Buck, Chris, and Jennifer Lee. 2013. Frozen. United States: Walt Disney Studios Motion Pictures.

Johnson, Barbara. The Best Devotions of Barbara Johnson (Best Devotions of Women S) (p.180). Zondervan. Kindle Edition.

Endnotes

1. "Provisional Suicide Deaths in the United States, 2022."
    Centers for Disease Control and Prevention, August 10,
    2023.
    https://www.cdc.gov/media/releases/2023/s0810-US-Suicid
    e-Deaths-2022.html.

About the author

Karisa Moore knows what it's like to cry out to God with groans words cannot express (Romans 8:26). Losing her son to suicide makes her a passionate resource as an author, blogger, podcaster, photographer, and soul-care speaker. She is expanding our mental health vocabulary to include Christ-centered hope. Karisa embraces life alongside her husband and two living children. She loves long hikes, photography, and great stories.

www.ingramcontent.com/pod-product-compliance
Lightning Source LLC
Chambersburg PA
CBHW051609120626
46551CB00014B/1732